KENT CC
CRICKET
An A–Z

Dean Hayes

DEDICATION

In memory of Cyril Walker, my father-in-law and a very good friend.

First published in 2002 by S. B. Publications,
19 Grove Road, Seaford, East Sussex BN25 1TP
Tel: 01323 893498

ISBN 1 85770 250 6

Designed and typeset by CGB, Lewes.
Tel: 01273 476622
Printed by Page Turn Ltd, Hove
Tel: 01273 821500

ABOUT THE AUTHOR

Dean Hayes is an experienced freelance sports writer specialising in football and cricket. He was educated at Hayward Grammar School, Bolton and West Midlands College of Physical Education, and was a Primary School Head Teacher until taking up writing on a permanent basis seven years ago.

He has played football in the Lancashire Amateur League, but he now concentrates solely on playing the summer game. This former cricket professional, now residing in the sunny climes of Pembrokeshire and playing as an amateur, has taken well over 2,000 wickets in league cricket.

Dean is married to Elaine and has one son and two stepchildren. This is his fifteenth book on cricket to be published — and his sixty-fifth overall.

ACKNOWLEDGEMENTS

The author would like to thank the following organisations for help in compiling this book: Kent County Cricket Club, the British Newspaper Library and the Harris Library. I would also like to thank Peter Stafford (ex-Bolton League Secretary) for his continued input into my cricket titles.

My gratitude also goes to the *Lancashire Evening Post* for providing the bulk of the photographs in this book, the remainder coming from my own personal collection.

SELECT BIBLIOGRAPHY

Arrowsmith R L. *Kent.* Arthur Barker 1971

Harris, Lord. *The History of Kent County Cricket Club.* Eyre and
          Spottiswoode 1906

Hayes, Dean. *Kent's Cricketing Greats.* Spellmont 1990

Kent CCC. *One Hundred Years of Kent Cricket 1870-1970*

Fowle, Dennis. *Kent: The Glorious Years 1967-1979*

Moore, Dudley. *The History of Kent CCC.* Christopher Helm 1989

Swanton and Taylor. *Kent Cricket; A Photographic History 1985*

ABANDONED MATCHES

Twenty of Kents County Championship matches have been abandoned. Sixteen of them were abandoned without a ball being bowled because of the weather; one match in 1910 was cancelled because of the death of King Edward VII; one match in 1926 was cancelled because of the General Strike and two matches in 1939 were cancelled because of the outbreak of war.

AMES, LES

One of the games finest wicketkeeper/batsmen, Les Ames made his Kent debut in 1926, replacing Jack Hubble as the countys wicketkeeper the following summer. In 1929 he set a wicketkeeping record which has stood unchallenged since and which will never be approached unless the organisation of first-class cricket is once again radically altered. He helped to dismiss 127 batsmen — 79 caught and 48 stumped — his best performance coming in the match against Sussex at Maidstone when he helped to dismiss nine batsmen. He was selected as one of *Wisden's* Five Cricketers of the Year.

He made his Test debut against South Africa at the Oval midway through the season, and he toured the West Indies in 1929-30, making his highest Test score of 149 at Kingston.

Having scored more than 1,000 runs in each of his first-class seasons, Ames topped the 2,000 run mark for the first time in 1931, scoring 2,100 runs at an average of 61.76. He scored three centuries in successive innings — 130 not out v Middlesex; 149 v Northamptonshire and 120 v Surrey. In 1933, Ames scored 3,058 runs in all first-class matches at an average of 58.80. He scored two double hundreds that summer — 210 v Warwickshire at Tonbridge and then the highest score of his career, 295 v Gloucestershire at Folkestone.

By nature he was an attacking player and this innings took him less than three-and-a-half hours. Twice before the war, Ames won the Lawrence Trophy for the quickest hundred of the season, the years being 1936 and 1938.

One of his best knocks came in the Lords Test of 1934 against Australia. When he joined Maurice Leyland, the Australians had England struggling somewhat at 182 for five. Together they added 129 — Leyland going for 109, Ames making 120. Verity, on a Lords wicket ruined by rain, took 15 for 104 and England won by an innings, but without Amess contribution the result could have been so different.

In 1935, during the Oval Test against South Africa, Ames scored the most runs ever made before lunch in a Test — 123. He started the morning on 25 not out, proceeding to 148 in magnificent fashion. In 1937 he again hit three centuries in successive innings — 125 v Worcestershire and then 119 and 127 in the same match against Surrey at Blackheath.

In his 47 Tests, Ames scored eight centuries. One of these, 115, was made in 1938-39 against South Africa when he shared a 137-run partnership with Wally Hammond. This remains a fourth wicket record between the two countries. His record as a batsman in Tests shows that he must have been a strong candidate for a place, even if he had never kept wicket, for he scored 2,434 runs at an average of 40.56.

After the war, Les Ames was batting just as well as he had prior to the hostilities. By 1949 he was the clubs senior professional and many Kent followers were mystified he was not appointed captain when Kent were looking for a successor to Bryan Valentine. In 1950 he hit hundreds in both innings of the match against Gloucestershire at Bristol, the third time he had achieved this feat. It was also the season that he scored his hundredth century, against Middlesex at Canterbury.

Shortly afterwards he broke down with back trouble and after scoring 29,851 runs at 44.33 and helping to dismiss 842 batsmen, he was forced to retire.

He was a Test selector from 1950 to 1956 and in 1958, and manager of Kent from 1957 to 1960. Then, until 1974, he combined the duties of manager and secretary. In 1975 he became the first ex-professional to be President of Kent, a well deserved honour.

APPEARANCES

The players with the highest number of first-class appearances for Kent are as follows:

Frank Woolley	764
Wally Hardinge	606
Jim Seymour	536
Derek Underwood	520
Tich Freeman	506
Bill Ashdown	482
Fred Huish	469
Les Ames	430
Leslie Todd	426
Arthur Fagg	414

ASHDOWN, BILL

The most unselfish and popular of cricketers, Bill Ashdown began to make his mark as a very sound batsman in the summer of 1921. He possessed a wide array of strokes and often bowled at a shade over medium-pace.

In 1926, Ashdown passed the 1,000 run mark for the first time, a feat he was to achieve, with the exception of 1932, from that summer until 1937. His best season in terms of runs scored was 1928 when he totalled 2,267 runs at an average of 43.21.

He formed a formidable opening partnership with Wally Hardinge, which became the foundation on which the stroke play of Ames and Woolley flourished.

Ashdowns innings of 332 against Essex on a pitch of unnatural ease, made out of Kents 803 for four, is one that many remember him by. His knock was in the first innings in the first Brentwood week of 1934. To elaborate further, Kents total of 803 was made in just over seven hours. Ashdown and Fagg put on 70 for the first wicket before Fagg departed and in walked Frank Woolley. He stayed a little more than three hours, making 172, and was out just after tea with the score on 422. Les Ames took strike and went on to hit an unbeaten 202. The score at the close of play on that first day was 623 for two. While all this was going on, Bill Ashdown had unselfishly accumulated 300 runs in a day, averaging 50 runs an hour off his own bat. He eventually fell for 332, Kent winning the game by an innings and 192 runs. He almost exceeded this score the following season when he carried his bat through an innings of 560 with a faultless 305 made against Derbyshire at Dover.

Although he went on to score 22,309 runs for Kent at an average of 30.64, Ashdown was a little too inconsistent and prone to spells of failure to be considered for England or other representative teams. He took 595 wickets with his useful bowling and held 398 catches, mostly at slip. He is also the only player to have played first-class cricket before the First World War and after the Second World War.

From 1938 to 1947, he was coach at Rugby, combining the post with being head groundsman. From his position at Rugby, Ashdown moved on to the first-class umpires panel and later became Leicestershires coach and scorer.

AUSTRALIA

At Canterbury in 1882, Kent met the Australians for the first time, losing by seven wickets. During the match, a presentation was made by the clubs president, the sixth Earl of Darnley to Lord Harris — the testimonial consisting of a pair of silver candelabra which cost 400 guineas. Two years later, Harris top-scored with 60 as Kent became the only county side to beat the Australians. In 1889, the Australians were beaten again by Kent with Leonard Hamilton carrying his bat to score 117 out of a total of 205 and Albert Daffen finishing off the tourists with four wickets for five runs.

In 1930 at Canterbury, Frank Woolley hit 60 in no time at all, the majority coming off Alan Fairfax, who on asking his skipper Vic Richardson if he thought it was all right bowling at his off stump? was told All right? Its bloody marvellous — we re all enjoying it.

The match against Australia at Canterbury in 1948, on Sir Donald Bradmans final tour, had special significance in more ways than one. The game was watched by crowds totalling almost 39,000 but Kent in their first innings were dismissed for 51, one short of Englands score in the Oval Test match. When Kent batted for a second time, a member offered £50 to the first batsman to make a half-century. Pawson and Evans were batting when the wicketkeeper, on 49, danced down the wicket to McCool and called for a single. Pawson, unaware of the reward offered, sent him back and Evans, who had hit the ball to Bradman, the only close fielder, kept on running straight to the pavilion.

Peter Richardson hit a century in each innings of the match against Australia in 1964, repeating the feat of Colin Cowdrey on the Australian s previous tour three years earlier.

Cowdrey s last century against the Australians came at Canterbury in 1975. Chasing 354 to win, at more than a run a minute, Cowdrey, with his match-winning innings of 151 not out, steered Kent to a four wicket victory. He was then forty-three years old and was hooking the ferocious Lillee in front of square.

Colin Cowdrey

B

BENSON, MARK

Mark Benson was thirteen when he first picked up a cricket bat. Cricket was just one of a number of sports that he enjoyed — rugby, hockey and tennis being the others. Benson's father was, however, keen for him to succeed in the game of cricket and sent him to Alf Gover's Indoor School for cricket coaching when he was fourteen years old.

The following summer he won a place in the School 1st XI and at the age of seventeen played against the Kent Schools, top-scoring with 90. He was then chosen for the Kent Schools and later for the Public Schools XI. In his early days with the Kent 2nd XI, he was also playing an important role in enabling his club side, Sevenoaks Vine, to win the Kent League.

He made his first-class debut in 1980 and, although he hit a couple of fifties, he had to wait until the following summer before making his maiden century against Warwickshire. Benson ended his first full season with 1,083 runs at an average of 32.31. Despite a bad finger injury ruling him out of a number of games in 1982 he still passed the 1,000 run mark, finishing with 1,100 runs at 44.00.

The following season was his best to date, his 1,515 runs including 102 and 152 not out in the match against Warwickshire at Edgbaston. His performances that summer led to his one and only appearance for England at Test level and he scored 21 and 30 against India at Edgbaston.

Over the next few seasons Benson continued to be a prolific scorer 'for Kent and in 1991 made his highest first-class score, 257 against Hampshire at Southampton.

Benson passed 1,000 runs in a season eleven times, with a best of 1,725 in 1987. He was Captain of Kent from 1991 to 1995 and he went on to score forty-eight centuries in a total of 18,284 runs at 40.27 before leaving the first-class game.

BENSON AND HEDGES CUP

Kent have been involved in eight Benson and Hedges Finals, their first against Worcestershire in 1973. Kents 225 for seven was made by a great partnership of 116 in 28 overs by Luckhurst and Asif Iqbal. The real feature of the partnership was the running between the wickets. Eventually, inevitably, Asif (59) ran Luckhurst (79) off his legs, but with Ealham, Shepherd, Cowdrey and Knott all chipping in, Kent totalled 225 for seven.

Worcestershires innings revolved round Giffords use of his left-handers, sent in out of order expressly to get after Underwood. However, he held D Oliveira back,and although he did score 47 from 48 balls, Asif s four for 43 to go with his half-century, saw him voted Man-of-the-Match as Kent won by 39 runs.

Kent joined Leicestershire in winning the Benson and Hedges Cup for a second time in 1976, defeating Worcestershire by 43 runs. The final was not an outstanding match except for a marvellous piece of cricket by Basil D Oliveira. Hobbling about on one leg he scored 50, Worcestershires highest individual score in a total of 193. But Kent had virtually controlled the day from the moment that Johnson and Woolmer put on 110 for the first wicket. Jarvis mopped up the Worcestershire tail to take four for 34 but it was Underwood who prised out the earlier batsmen to prove what a splendid bowler he was, even in one-day cricket. Graham Johnson, for his innings of 78, which gave the Kent bowlers a total to bowl at, was named Man-of-the-Match.

Kent returned to Lords again the following year for the Benson and Hedges Final against Gloucestershire. At one time, Gloucestershire were 144 for one and though they did not really build the huge total which seemed likely, the 237 they did score was far too much for Kent. Only Woolmer (64) and Shepherd (56) showed any form as Kent were bowled out for 173.

In 1978 Kent won the Benson and Hedges Cup for the third time, in only seven years of the competition, by a comprehensive victory over Derbyshire. At one time Derbyshire were going quite well at 121 for four, but they collapsed totally to be all out for 147. Kent won by six wickets, Woolmer with 79 dominated Kents batting and was made Man-of-the-Match by chairman of England selectors, Alec Bedser. John Shepherd

11

Benson and Hedges 1995 Man-of-the-Match Aravinda de Silva.

also had a good match, taking four for 25 in eleven overs, scoring 19 not out and catching Kirsten, top-scorer in the Derbyshire side.

Eight years elapsed before Kent returned to Lords for their fifth Benson and Hedges Final. They won a vital toss on a morning of such mist and mirk that most pundits were predicting either the pre-lunch loss of eight wickets or the total abandonment of play. At lunch, Middlesex were 89 for four but Radley and Downton and some lusty blows from Emburey saw Middlesex s innings close on 199 for seven. Kent struggled from the word go until Graham Cowdrey hit a swashbuckling 58 to give them a fighting chance. However, at 7.32 pm in near darkness and steady drizzle, Middlesex won an extraordinary final when Dilley failed to hit the final ball from Hughes for six.

Kents sixth appearance in a Benson and Hedges Final, in 1982, saw them beaten by Hampshire. All of Hampshires batsmen got amongst the runs but Robin Smith led the way with 90. Their total of 253 for five was a fairly formidable one and though Kent made a go of things, they fell 41 runs short, Mark Benson top-scoring with 59.

In spite of Aravinda de Silva winning the Man-of-the-Match award for his brilliant innings of 112 in the Benson and Hedges Final of 1995, Kent lost to Lancashire by 35 runs. At one stage Lancashire were 201 for one, finally ending their innings on 274 for seven. Unfortunately for Kent, nobody could stay with de Silva, the next highest scorers being Fulton and Graham Cowdrey who both made 25.

Kents last appearance in a Benson and Hedges Final was in 1997 when they were completely overwhelmed by Surrey, who won by eight wickets. Kent were restricted to 212 for nine in their fifty overs and although McCague had an early success with the wicket of Ally Brown, Stewart and Ben Hollioake, who fell two runs short of his hundred, dominated proceedings. Kents Benson and Hedges Cup records include:

Highest Innings Total	338 for six v Somerset at Maidstone 1996
Lowest Innings Total	73 v Middlesex at Canterbury 1979
Highest Individual Score	143 by Chris Tavare v Somerset at Taunton 1985
Best Bowling Performance	6 for 41 by Tim Wren v Somerset at Canterbury 1995
Highest Partnership	229 by Trevor Ward and Mark Benson for the 1st wicket v Surrey at Canterbury 1995

BEST XI

Selecting a best team can be a fascinating relaxation but it can also be highly provocative, for players were at their best in different decades. Comparisons can be odious and the more one thinks of all the players who have represented Kent the more difficult the task of selecting the best eleven becomes. It was not easy to leave out players of the calibre of Godfrey Evans, Doug Wright and Asif Iqbal, but below is my best Kent team.

Les Ames	Alan Knott
Arthur Fagg	Arthur Fielder
Colin Cowdrey	Colin Blythe
Wally Hardinge	Derek Underwood
Jack Mason	Tich Freeman
Frank Woolley	

BLACKHEATH

Kent has always been noted for the loveliness of its cricket grounds and the Rectory Field at Blackheath, though claiming none of the idyllic beauty of Mote Park or the Nevill Ground, always provided a friendly scene of trees and marquees amid the austerity of South East London. Here, too, the first Rugby international was played between England and Wales in 1880-81.

The Rectory Field has staged some of Kents most intriguing battles with Surrey, their traditional visitors. Here, in 1919, Frank Woolley achieved the hat-trick and in 1934 Tich Freeman repeated the feat. But perhaps the most remarkable performance came in 1956 when Tony Lock took all ten Kent wickets for 54 runs.

Blackheath abounds with historic batting feats. In 1921 Wally Hardinge scored 207 and 102 not out against Surrey. In the same match, Shepherd exceeded Hardinges first innings performance with 210 not out. The match against Essex in 1951 was an incredible one. Essex, after declaring at 435 for five and needing 126 to win in three-quarters of an hour when they batted again, lost seven wickets for 13 runs as the game ended in a draw.

Colin Cowdrey made Kents highest score on the ground in 1959 when he hit 250 against Surrey.

BLYTHE, COLIN

As a slow left-arm bowler, Colin Blythe dominated Edwardian cricket and earned his place among the greatest bowlers of all-time. Only once, in the fourteen seasons that followed his Kent debut in 1899, did he fail to take 100 wickets in a season. That was in 1901 when his health was poor, but even then his tally was 97 wickets.

He visited Australia with a team captained by Archie MacLaren in 1901-02 and never looked back. Over the next three seasons he took 398 wickets, with Hampshire being the county to suffer most. In 1904 he had match figures of thirteen for 91 at Southampton (including nine for 30 in the first innings) following it up with fifteen for 76 at Tonbridge.

In May 1907 he accomplished the remarkable performance of taking ten wickets in an innings and seventeen in a match — all in one day at Northampton. At one time, Northamptonshire were 4 runs for seven wickets, Blythe having taken seven Northamptonshire wickets for one run. They managed to make 60 in their first innings, faring even worse in the second when they were all out for 39. Blythe emerged as the conquering hero with ten for 30 and seven for 18 — all in less than a days play during 31.1 overs.

In the same season he played in all three Tests against South Africa. The first and third Tests were drawn but the second at Headingley was a different affair on a pitch that was affected by rain. England were dismissed for 76 and South Africa could only muster 110, Blythe taking eight for 59. In their second innings, England made 162, leaving South Africa to make 129 to win. They did not stand a chance as Blythe never bowled a loose delivery, finishing with seven for 40, and South Africa were all out for 75. Altogether that season, Blythe took 183 wickets at an average of 15.42 runs each.

Charlie , as he was always called, was an accomplished violinist, and there was certainly something of this in his bowling. His long sensitive musicians fingers enabling him to spin the ball and make it leap from the pitch as if it, the ball, were alive. As a complete contrast to his love for the violin, he would also willingly pay five guineas to see a good fight.

Blythe found games for Kent no trouble, but it is said that he found that Test matches got on his nerves . The series against Australia in 1909, and especially the match at Edgbaston, was a prime example. In that match, Blythe took eleven for 102 but on his return to Kent a medical specialist advised the county club that he should not play in the next Test at Lords. The consultants diagnosis was that Blythe suffered in a peculiar way from the strain on his nervous system caused by playing in a Test match . Instead of playing at Lords he continued to represent Kent, taking thirty-six wickets in the space of twelve days.

His best season was 1909 when he took 215 wickets in all first-class matches at a cost of 14.54 runs apiece. In one day at Leicester he took fourteen for 56 (including nine for 42 in the first innings). In his career, Blythe took 2,509 wickets at an average cost of 16.80 runs each.

In 1914 he was bowling as well as ever and for the third year running he topped the first-class bowling averages. He was one of the first cricket professionals to join up and sometime in 1917, Sgt Colin Blythe announced that he was taking up a coaching appointment at Eton and he would retire from county cricket. Those plans never came to fruition, for in November of that year he was killed by a shell after being drafted to the Western Front.

BRADLEY, WALTER

Bill Bradley was a tall, hard-working right-handed fast bowler, who possessed such stamina that he could maintain considerable pace for long periods from an exceptionally long approach.

After captaining Alleyns School and once taking six Mitcham wickets with consecutive balls for Lloyds Register, he was taken under Lord Harriss wing and began to play for Kent as an amateur. He made his Kent debut in 1895 but it was four years later before he made his mark. In 1899, Bradley took 129 wickets in the Championship at a cost of 17.91 runs each. He also performed the hat-trick on two occasions, the first against Essex at Leyton and the second against Yorkshire at Tonbridge.

Also that year he represented England on two occasions against the Australians. The game at Old Trafford was proof of his ability to bowl spells without losing his pace — his great efforts bringing him the figures of five for 67 off 33 overs. Under the laws of that time Australia had to follow-on, and Bill Bradley went on to bowl a further 46 overs. In all matches that season, his victims totalled 156 at an average of 19.10. He was by far the best amateur bowler that year.

In 1900, Bradley performed the hat-trick for the third time, against Somerset at Blackheath, and in the following summer he recorded his best figures for the county, nine for 37 against Hampshire at Tonbridge. In nine seasons of first-class cricket, he took 624 wickets at 22.64 runs each.

In the last few years of his life, which coincided with the Second World War, he would wear his MCC tie and visit the Long Room at Lords to talk over past matches.

BROTHERS

There have been a number of instances of brothers playing for the county. George (1875-1895) and Alec (1884-1906) Hearne both played for Kent and both made one Test appearance for England in the match against South Africa at Cape Town in W W Reads tour of 1891-92. George Hearne scored 7,148 runs and took 569 wickets for Kent and his younger brother, Alec, scored 13,598 runs and captured 1,018 wickets.

Samuel Day (1897-1919) scored 5,893 runs for Kent and brother Arthur (1905-1925) amassed 6,532 runs, including holding the county record seventh wicket partnership when he and Edward Humphreys put on 248 against Somerset at Taunton in 1908.

In the match against Northamptonshire at Northampton in 1913, there was the unusual sight of two Kent players in direct opposition to their brothers. At one stage, C N Woolley and John Seymour were batting against their respective brothers, Frank and James.

In 1921 Tich Freeman was too good for his brother, Jack, for when Kent played Essex at Leyton and later in the season at Tunbridge Wells, the Kent bowler dismissed him in both matches.

The most famous set of brothers to play for Kent in recent years has been Chris and Graham Cowdrey. Chris, who played in six Test matches for England, scored 11,948 runs for the hop county and Graham totalled 8,213.

BURNUP, CUTHBERT

After playing his early cricket for Malvern School, Cuthbert Burnup moved on to Cambridge University, playing on a regular basis from 1896 to 1898. During that first season, he scored 666 runs in just nine innings, including 80 at Lords in the match against Oxford University. It was during this match W G Grace was dismissed without scoring in both innings and Cambridge bowler, E B Shine, acting on his captains orders, deliberately bowled three balls to the boundary to prevent Oxford following-on.

In 1899, after joining Kent three years earlier, Burnup scored 1,557 runs at an average of 44.48. In the match against Surrey at the Oval, he carried his bat, scoring 103 not out in Kent's total of 209. The following year he made the highest score of his career, 200 against Lancashire at Old Trafford. At that time, it was also the highest ever made for Kent.

Burnup had a busy style, tending to score runs quicker than the spectator realised. He played well off his legs, though he favoured the cut and off-drive. His stance was similar to Gilbert Jessop of Gloucestershire. Holding the bat low, he would await delivery in a crouched position. Like other players of his generation, he was a good soccer player, winning full international honours for England when he played against Scotland in 1896. The majority of his games were, however, for the Corinthians.

In 1903 he was appointed captain of Kent, a position he kept until they captured the County Championship in 1906. In that year, Burnup scored 1,207 runs at an average of 67.05.

When he retired from the first-class scene the following year he had scored 9,668 runs at an average of 38.06, higher than that of any other regular player.

CAPTAINS

This is the complete list of Kents captains:

1871-1874	Various	1937	R T Bryan and
1875-1889	Lord Harris		B H Valentine
1890-1893	F Marchant and	1938-1939	F G H Chalk
	W H Patterson	1946-1948	B H Valentine
1894-1897	F Marchant	1949-1951	D G Clark
1898-1902	J R Mason	1952-1953	W Murray-Wood
1903	C J Burnup	1954-1956	D V P Wright
1904-1908	C H B Marsham	1957-1971	M C Cowdrey
1909-1913	E W Dillon	1972-1976	M H Denness
1914-1923	L H W Troughton	1977	Asif Iqbal
1924-1926	W S Cornwallis	1978-1980	A G E Ealham
1927	A J Evans	1981-1982	Asif Iqbal
1928-1930	G B Legge	1983-1984	C J Tavare
1931-1935	A P F Chapman	1985-1990	C S Cowdrey
	and B H Valentine	1991-1995	M R Benson
1936	A P F Chapman,	1996-1998	S A Marsh
	B H Valentine and	1999-	M V Fleming
	I S Akers-Douglas		

CAMBRIDGE UNIVERSITY

When Kent played Cambridge University at Fenners in 1958, South African-born all-rounder Stuart Leary equalled the county record by taking six catches in one innings.

CANTERBURY

The St Lawrence Cricket Ground was opened in 1847 and was known at that time as the Beverley Cricket Ground, a name that came from a ground which was used by the club from 1841 to 1846. The current name comes from the adjoining St Lawrence House, originally the St Lawrence Priory. The St Lawrence ground is the only cricket ground in Kent that is owned by the county club. The first match there was in 1847 when Kent beat England by three wickets but it was not until 1896 that the county club bought the freehold.

The highest innings — perhaps even the best on the ground — was 344 by W G Grace for MCC v Kent in 1876. It was after playing this innings that Grace went on to score 177 v Nottinghamshire at Clifton and 318 not out v Yorkshire at Cheltenham in his next two innings — a record of 839 runs in three consecutive innings which still stands.

Another memorable innings on the St Lawrence ground was Joe Hardstaff s 126 for Nottinghamshire in 1937. Needing 310 to win in three hours, the visitors won with 45 minutes to spare after Hardstaff had scored 117 out of 134 for the third wicket in an hour. Completing his century in only 51 minutes, Hardstaff won the Lawrence Trophy for that season.

In 1949, Doug Wright achieved the hat-trick against Hampshire and set up a new world record, as it was the seventh of his first-class career.

E M Grace, playing for MCC v Gentlemen of Kent in 1862, took all ten wickets at a cost of 92 runs in the second innings following an innings of 192 not out when he carried his bat through the MCC innings of 344. It so happened that E M Grace was not at that time a member of the MCC but was allowed to play by Kent — by the end of the match they were no doubt regretting their hospitality.

CARR, DOUGLAS

On leaving Oxford University, where he played little cricket because of an injury to his knee he picked up playing football, Douglas Carr moved to Kent. Here he began to play club cricket for Mote Park, the Free Foresters and the Band of Brothers. By 1908 he had developed the ability to bowl both the googly and the leg-break and his performances in club cricket alerted Kent.

He was thirty-seven when he made his Kent debut against Oxford University in 1909, taking five for 65 in the first innings. On the strength of this one match, he was asked to play for the Gentlemen against the Players — having match figures of eight for 138 at Lords and seven for

128 at the Oval. His County Championship debut for Kent came later that year when he took six for 85 against Essex at Leyton.

Towards the end of the season he was chosen to represent his country against the Australians in the Oval Test match. His captain, Archie MacLaren, was heavily criticised in some quarters for bowling Carr into the ground — he finished with five for 146 in the first innings. Carr was MacLarens secret weapon and for a time it worked but Carr never played for his country again, neither did poor MacLaren.

At the end of the season Carr took eight for 105 for Lord Londesboroughs XI against the Australians and for his performances throughout the summer, he was chosen as one of *Wisden's* Five Cricketers of the Year.

Carr, who was a schoolmaster, continued to play county cricket for Kent during the holidays, contributing greatly to the county winning the Championship three times in five years. In the six seasons he played for Kent, Carr took 334 wickets at an average of 16.84 runs each. He had showed the Kent committee the value of a leg-break and googly bowler and was probably instrumental in them signing Tich Freeman.

CATCHES

The most catches in an innings by a Kent player is six, a feat achieved by two county players — James Seymour v South Africa at Canterbury in 1904 and Stuart Leary v Cambridge University at Fenners in 1958.

Chris Tavare holds the county record for the most catches in a season with 48 in 1978, and Frank Woolley holds the Kent record for the most catches in a career with 773 between 1906 and 1938.

CENTURIES

There have been eight players who have scored a century on their debut for Kent. They are Samuel Day who was 101 not out v Gloucestershire at Cheltenham in 1897; Jack Bryan, 124 v Nottinghamshire at Trent Bridge in 1920; Arthur Evans, 102 v Northamptonshire at Northampton in 1921; Alan Hilder, 103 not out v Essex at Gravesend in 1924; Peter Hearn, 124 v Warwickshire at Gillingham in 1947; Neil Taylor, 110 v Sri Lanka at Canterbury in 1979; Derek Aslett, 146 not out v Hampshire at

Bournemouth in 1981; and Carl Hooper, 115 not out v Durham at Canterbury in 1992.

There have been three occasions when four Kent players scored centuries in one innings — against Somerset at Taunton in 1908 (E Humphreys 149, J Seymour 129, A Day 118 and F Woolley 105 in a total of 601 for eight declared); v Oxford University at the Parks in 1982 (B Woolmer 126, N Taylor 127, C Tavare 125 and M Benson 120 in a total of 616 for six declared) and again v Oxford University at the Parks in 1988 (S Hinks 138, R Pienaar 127, C Tavare 138 not out and C S Cowdrey 124 not out in a total of 539 for three declared). This feat has never been performed against Kent.

The most centuries in a season by an individual player is ten, a total achieved by Frank Woolley in seasons 1928 and 1934.

Both Wally Hardinge and Frank Woolley scored four centuries in successive innings. Hardinge achieved the feat in 1913, scoring 154 not out v Leicestershire at Canterbury, 117 and 105 not out v Hampshire at Dover and 107 v Northamptonshire at Dover. Woolley followed suit in 1929, scoring 155 v Derbyshire at Chesterfield, 108 v Somerset at Tonbridge, 131 v Yorkshire at Tonbridge and 117 v Hampshire at Folkestone.

Seventeen players have scored a century in each innings of a match with Les Ames and Wally Hardinge having done so on three occasions. The first person to achieve the feat was Kenneth Hutchings in 1907 when he scored 109 and 109 not out v Worcestershire at New Road. The last person to score a century in each innings was Aravinda de Silva in 1995 when he hit 255 and 116 in the game against Derbyshire at Maidstone.

Arthur Fielder scored 112 not out at No.11 in 1909 against Worcestershire — one of only three instances of a No.11 making a first-class century in the Championship.

The following players have scored the most centuries for Kent:

Frank Woolley	122	Jim Seymour	53
Les Ames	78	Mark Benson	48
Wally Hardinge	73	Neil Taylor	42
Colin Cowdrey	58	Brian Luckhurst	39
Arthur Fagg	55	Bill Ashdown	38

CHALK, GERRY

After topping his school batting averages at Uppingham, Gerry Chalk moved up to Oxford University where he gained his Blue in 1931. He never appeared on the losing side in Oxford-Cambridge confrontations with his best performance being a magnificent 108 at Lords in 1934. On coming down from Oxford, Chalk spent a couple of years as a master at Malvern and so his scholastic duties somewhat limited his appearances for Kent.

Chalk had a very skilful defence but he could also score at every available opportunity, making him a valuable asset to have at your disposal. In 1937, while still not devoting his entire time to Kent cricket, he scored a superb 107 in a fighting innings at Lords against Middlesex. He cut, drove and pulled his way to a century on a badly worn pitch, hitting three sixes and ten fours. It was not until 1938 that he was available for a full season and then he was made captain. He made 1,057 runs and shared in a second wicket stand of 275 with Arthur Fagg in the match against Worcestershire at Dudley.

The following summer, Chalk made his highest score of 198 against Sussex at Tonbridge, though probably his greatest effort came in the match against Yorkshire at Dover just a week before the outbreak of the Second World War. Kent were forced to follow-on and in their second innings were dismissed for 215. Despite losing the match, Gerry Chalk carried his bat for a magnificent 115 not out.

Gerry Chalk was a good captain, getting the best out of all his players, but when war broke out he had not reached the peak of his performance, having scored just 4,436 runs at 28.25.

He joined the Honourable Artillery Company as a gunner before transferring to the RAF as a rear gunner. In June 1941 he won the DFC for the part he played when under attack returning from an air raid on Hanover. After taking a pilots course, he was promoted to Flight Lieutenant and later became a Spitfire Flight Commander. Chalk, who was a fine pianist, despite not being able to read a line of music, was reported missing in action in February 1943 and the following January was officially presumed killed . His tragic death, at the age of only thirty-two, was a tremendous blow to Kent County Cricket Club.

CHAMPIONSHIPS

Kent have won the County Championship on six occasions outright and shared the title with Middlesex in 1977. Their first success came in 1906 when they gained a victory that, according to Lengs *Cricket Handbook of 1907,* was extraordinarily popular, a result due to the brilliant character of their play and their splendid sportsmanship . In fact, Kent won the title again in 1909,1910 and 1913. Six players — Blythe, Fielder, Fairservice, Seymour, Humphreys and Huish — were regular members of the XI in all four Championship years and Mason, Hutchings, Woolley and Dillon played in three of them.

The outstanding bowler in the historic 1906 success was Arthur Fielder who, with immense help from Fred Huish behind the stumps and with Hutchings, Seymour and Mason almost infallible in the slips, took 158 Championship wickets. The batting that season was headed by Cuthbert Burnup but the most dazzling player was Ken Hutchings.

Marsham captained Kent to their first title but Edward Dillon led the side to their other successes.

In 1909, Jack Mason headed the national batting averages and Colin Blythe s 178 wickets in the Championship cost just 14.07 runs apiece. Twice he took nine wickets in an innings — nine for 42 v Leicestershire and nine for 44 v Northamptonshire. Kent retained the title the following year. Hutchings and Humphreys were in fine form with the bat, the latter making an unbeaten 200 against Lancashire at Tunbridge Wells.

Blythe took 149 wickets at only 13.70, but it was Douglas Carr, with 60 wickets at 12.16, who topped the national bowling averages.

When Kent won the title for a fourth time in 1913, Frank Woolley had a splendid all-round season, scoring 1,507 runs at 43.05 and taking 83 wickets at 17.61. Colin Blythe continued to be the county s most prolific wicket-taker, his 145 wickets at 15.54 runs each, placing him at the top of the national averages. Fred Huish was the country s leading wicketkeeper with eighty-four dismissals.

There was a gap of fifty-seven years before Kent won the title again in 1970, their centenary year. They did so despite losing most of their leading players at various stages of the season — Cowdrey, Denness, Luckhurst, Knott and Underwood all representing England at Test level.

Kents fielding played a decisive part in their climb from the bottom of the table in July. By September with two matches to play, they were in second place. They then beat Leicestershire by an innings and rivals Glamorgan and Lancashire played out an exciting drawn match at Cardiff. Kent tackled Surrey at the Oval and a drawn match ensured that the Championship was theirs.

In 1977 Kent shared the Championship title with Middlesex. Both sides were affected by the calls upon their players for Test cricket, but Kents loss of Underwood, Knott and Woolmer, who headed the national averages with 19 wickets at 15.21 apiece, definitely made the difference between sharing the title and winning it outright.

Kent last won the Championship in 1978. It had been suggested that with their Packer players available all season they ought to finish on top. Their success reflected great credit on Alan Ealham, who captained the county in the place of Asif Iqbal. Young players were given their chances and Underwood had a marvellous season, taking 110 wickets at a cost of 14.49.

CHAPMAN, PERCY

No amateur brought a more refreshing outlook to his cricket or had a more intense abhorrence of defensive play than Percy Chapman. He went to Uppingham School and was in its 1st XI for four years from 1916 to 1919, the last two as captain. In 1917 he topped the school batting averages, scoring 668 runs in just ten innings and an average of 111.33. His adventurous left-handed batting and fielding won him a Blue at Cambridge as a freshman. This was not too surprising, especially as on his first-class debut he had taken 118 off the Essex attack at Fenners.

Chapman had been playing well for Berkshire in Minor County cricket but in 1924 he qualified for Kent by taking a job in Mackesons Brewery in Hythe. He was one of the few players to play for England while still playing Minor County cricket. His England debut was in 1924 against South Africa at home, followed by the trip to Australia under A E R Gilligan. From then onwards he was a permanent fixture in the England team, captaining his country on seventeen occasions.

In 1926 he was to become a national hero as he led England to victory at the Oval and the Ashes were regained.

Chapmans greatest innings came in 1927. Kent were playing champions

Lancashire at Maidstone and when he marched to the wicket, they were struggling at 70 for five. Percy Chapman and Geoff Legge added 284 in two-and-a-half hours. Legges contribution was 101 but it was Chapman with 260 who turned it Kents way.

He only hit one century for England — 121 against Australia at Lords in 1930. With that he achieved a triple performance never before accomplished. He had previously hit hundreds for Cambridge and then in 1922 for the Gentlemen against the Players, a match in which Chapman had made nineteen appearances.

Chapman captained Kent from 1931 to 1936. In that capacity he was often criticised for not being a great tactician but one thing was certain— all those who played under him were happy and cheerful for he was a generous and carefree character.

In his entire career, Chapman scored 16,309 runs at an average of 31.97. Figures, however, do not give a true picture of this hard-hitting batsman who could turn a game as quickly as any cricketer of his generation or since.

After the Second World War his life went into sad eclipse. His health grew so bad that he could not get to Lords or Canterbury to watch the game he loved so much. He died in Alton Hospital, aged sixty-one, a player who will always be remembered for his great personal charm.

COLLINS, GEORGE

George Collins father and uncle played for Kent in the early 1880s, his father Christopher having the honour of playing for Cobham under the captaincy of the Honourable Ivo Bligh, eighth Earl of Darnley, who captained England on their successful trip to Australia in 1882.

George Collins only made a handful of appearances for Kent in the years leading up to the First World War and though he produced some brave innings, there seemed little chance of a regular spot and he left the staff. However, he returned in 1919.

In 1924 Kent were playing Yorkshire at Hull and trying to bat out for a draw. George Collins played a ball down to Maurice Leyland, fielding at short leg, who took it low to the ground claiming a catch. The umpire was unsighted and went to discuss the appeal with his colleague. The

Yorkshire team joined in the discussion, expressing their views in no uncertain terms. George, a friendly soul, left his crease to put forward his opinion. A Yorkshireman then removed the bails saying You re out now . The umpire, however, declared the catch a good one. When the matter was reported to Lord Harris, there was no sympathy for George Collins.

As a bowler, Collins would often capture valuable wickets early in the innings and certainly surprised one or two of the stronger county sides as he ran through them. Perhaps the best example of this occurred at Dover in 1922 when Nottinghamshire were the visitors. In the first innings he took six for 18 following it with all ten wickets in the second — ten for 65.

Despite his huge frame and his ability to lift a pavilion chair in his teeth and hold it parallel to the ground, he was rather a slow mover. In this match, when he had taken nine wickets, he had the chance to catch a ball from Tich Freeman s bowling that would have been the tenth wicket. He was slow to move to it and when he got there he could not hold on to it. He was greatly upset, suspecting that the crowd would think he had dropped it on purpose. In the following over it was Freeman who took a brilliant catch to provide Collins with all ten wickets.

COWDREY, CHRIS

The eldest of Colin Cowdrey s three sons, Chris Cowdrey was an aggressive, predominantly onside, middle-order batsman, right-arm medium-pace swing bowler and a quite exceptional fielder.

Chris Cowdrey s first Championship century against Glamorgan at Swansea in 1977 not only helped Kent towards a six-wicket victory but also allowed him to achieve something his father had never done and that was to score a century against the Welsh county.

Following Asif Iqbal s decision to relinquish the captaincy, the choice to replace him was between Chris Tavare and Chris Cowdrey. The issue was resolved by the appointment of Tavare to lead the side with Cowdrey to skipper the team when he was absent. Cowdrey spent some time considering his future and there was speculation that he might leave to captain another county. He decided to stay and in 1983 had a marvellous season, scoring 1,256 runs at 54.60 and finishing seventh in the national batting averages.

Chris Cowdrey in action with the bat.

Although injuries hampered his progress in 1984, he did enough to gain selection for the England tour of India. He played in all five Tests, performing usefully but not really asserting himself.

He was appointed Kents captain in 1985 and he started the season superbly, scoring 159 and 95 in the match against Surrey at Canterbury. Over the next few seasons, Cowdrey proved to be an inspired leader, whose enthusiasm and charisma lifted a rather mediocre Kent team to within one point of the 1988 Championship — an effort which included a notable sequence of six successive victories. In that summer of 1988 he was awarded the England captaincy for the last two Tests against the West Indies, but a foot injury forced him to withdraw before the second match and he was replaced by Graham Gooch, who retained the post for the subsequent Sri Lankan Test and aborted winter tour.

Chris Cowdrey s brief elevation completed only the second father and son captaincy double for England after Frank and George Mann.

Chris Cowdrey went on to score 11,869 runs at 32.42 before leaving the county in 1991 to see out his first-class career with Glamorgan.

COWDREY, COLIN

Colin Cowdrey was a most graceful and prolific batsman of the highest class whose timing was so immaculate that he appeared to caress the ball to the boundary.

His fathers enthusiasm for the game — he was, in fact, top-scorer for the Europeans against the 1926-27 touring team in India — led him to give his son the initials MCC. Colin Cowdrey was the youngest player to take part in a public schools match at Lords. In 1945 at the age of thirteen, he played for Tonbridge against Clifton. Classed as a leg-spin bowler, he batted at No.3 and in the first innings scored 75, which was more than half his sides total, following it up with 44 out of 175 in the second. As a bowler he took three for 58 in the first innings and then just as Clifton looked likely to win, he took their last five wickets for 33 to help Tonbridge win by two runs For the next five years he was to dominate cricket at Tonbridge School. He was so successful that he was chosen to captain the Public Schools XI against the Combined Services and scored a century. At the age of seventeen he was in the Kent side, and within two years he had been capped — the youngest to be so in Kents history.

He went up to Oxford, where he was a prolific scorer and a Blue for three years. He hit a hundred in the Varsity match and was captain in his last year.

Cowdrey was part of the 1954 MCC touring party to Australia. He batted quite usefully in the first two tests and hit two hundreds in the match against New South Wales but it was in the third Test at Melbourne that he produced one of the finest innings seen in a Test match. England were 41 for four with Edrich, May, Hutton and Compton back in the tent, as he made his way out to the middle. He went on to make 102 out of an all-out total of 191. Australia replied to Englands total with 231. England scored 279 in their second innings before Frank Tyson (seven for 27) bowled Australia out for 111 to give England victory by 128 runs.

At Edgbaston in 1957 came the turning point in Cowdreys development as a major Test batsman. He scored 154 against the West Indies as he and Peter May put on 411 for the fourth wicket in a little over eight hours. It was really the first time he had scored a Test hundred by occupation of the crease rather than by his usual magnificent stroke play. In 1959 he hit his highest score for Kent, 250 in the match against Essex at Blackheath.

During the MCC tour of the West Indies in 1959-60, Cowdrey played as an opener and had a wonderful time. His hooking of Wes Hall was brilliant. In ten innings he scored 491 runs at an average of 54.55, including 114 and 97 in the third Test at Kingston and 119 at Port of Spain.

In 1961, playing for Kent against the touring Australians, Cowdrey scored 149 and 121 as his side finished just eight runs short of their first win against the Australians since 1899.

The highest score of his career, 307, was made for the MCC team when they played South Australia in 1962-63. In 1963 his arm was broken in the Lords Test in mid-June but he bounced back the following summer with 1,562 runs at an average of 57.85.

Cowdrey s best domestic season was 1965 when he headed Kent s batting averages with 1,230 runs at 64.73. He also took hundreds off both the touring sides. In 1967-68 he captained England when they toured the West Indies. He batted magnificently on that tour and his innings of 71 at Port of Spain won the Test. The following summer saw Colin play his hundredth Test match, against the Australians at Edgbaston celebrating with yet another Test century.

One morning in December 1974, Colin Cowdrey s usual morning routine was shattered by a telephone call from Mike Denness in Australia. Injuries had ravaged the touring party and Colin, aged forty-two, was needed to join the rest of the party in their battle against Lillee and Thomson. He responded with skill and character and although he retired the following year, he managed to score his last century against the Australians — his innings of 151 not out steering Kent to victory by four wickets.

He made twenty-two Test centuries in a total of 7,624 runs at an average of 44.06, and for Kent he scored 23,779 runs at 42.01.

In 1986, Colin Cowdrey s appointment as MCC president for the country s bi-centenary in 1987 was well received by all connected with Kent cricket. Later he chaired the International Cricket Council, was knighted in 1992 and raised to the peerage five years later. Lord Cowdrey of Tonbridge was a true sportsman, charming, gentle and friendly. He was true to himself and to the game he loved, the ideal and happy cricketer for Kent and England.

COWDREY, GRAHAM

It was towards the end of the 1984 season when Graham Cowdrey forced his way into the Kent 1st XI on the back of big scores in the county's second team. Cowdrey, who captained the 2nd XI in 1984, broke the county record the following year with 1,300 runs in twenty-six innings for the 2nd XI.

Graham Cowdrey.

The younger Cowdrey brother first earned national recognition for his part in the Benson and Hedges Cup Final of 1986 when his heroic 58 from just seventy balls in fading light took Kent to the brink of a historic victory against Middlesex.

Cowdrey often produced his best performances with the bat for Kent in adversity, though as his career unfolded, he managed to find the consistency that was needed at this level. An outstanding fielder in any position with an accurate arm and a safe pair of hands, his bowling improved steadily, particularly in the one-day competitions where he was used with greater frequency.

In 1995 he and Aravinda de Silva created a new Kent record for any wicket when they added 368 runs for the fourth wicket against Derbyshire at Maidstone.

A member of the Christians in Sport organisation, Graham Cowdrey spent fourteen seasons playing first team cricket for Kent, scoring 8,858 runs at 34.73 and a top score of 147 against Gloucestershire at Bristol in 1992.

DARTFORD

Hesketh Park is the third ground to be used by Kent for home matches in the town. The long-established Dartford CC originally played on the Brent ground but it is one of the sporting tragedies of the town that in 1905, after the club had lost a lawsuit, the historic ground was sold for building development. Fortunately for the club, Everard Hesketh, a well known local figure, gave the Hesketh Park ground for the free use of the inhabitants of Dartford for ever . The first match played there was in 1906 between the *Daily Telegraph* XI and the Riverside Mills XI. Hesketh was accorded the honour of bowling the first over on the ground.

Kent first used the ground in May 1956 when Essex were the visitors and won by nine wickets, with Insole and Bailey both making centuries, Generally the wicket tends to favour the seamer and Fred Ridgway returned some good figures from Hesketh. In 1958 he and Brown shattered Somerset with a six for 16 spell and his eight for 39 helped to defeat Lancashire in 1960.

DEATH

Colin Blythe was killed at Ypres on 8 November 1917 at the age of thirty-eight. He had volunteered for active service on the outbreak of the First World War and was enrolled in the Kent Fortress Engineers. He was quickly promoted to sergeant and in 1917 was transferred to the Kings Own Yorkshire Light Infantry with which he was serving when he was killed in action.

A year earlier Ken Hutchings of the 4th Battalion the Kings Liverpool Regiment was also killed in battle during the First World War.

Gerry Chalk joined the Honourable Artillery Company as a gunner before transferring to the RAF as a rear gunner. He was reported missing after an operation in February 1943 and in January of the following year he was officially presumed killed .

South African all-rounder Stuart Leary was found dead on his beloved Table Mountain, four days after his abandoned car had been found. It was an untimely death and a sad end for a cricketer who had brought much pleasure to Kent supporters.

DEBUTS

Samuel Day became the first player in the clubs history to score a century on his debut. He was 101 not out in the second innings of the match against Gloucestershire at Cheltenham in 1896.

Although he only played in nine matches for Kent, in three seasons with the county, Percival Morfee had a remarkable debut. In 1910, he bowled Plum Warner twice in a day for a duck, with the third ball in the first innings and the first in the second.

Bill Ashdown, who went on to score 22,309 runs for Kent at an average of 30.64, made his first-class debut in 1914 for Mr G J V Weigalls XI against Oxford University at the age of fifteen, the youngest player ever to appear in a first-class game in England.

DEFEATS

Kents heaviest defeat came in 1898 in the match against Surrey at the Oval when they lost by an innings and 345 runs.

DENNESS, MIKE

Mike Denness played his early cricket for Ayr where his consistent batting displays made him the first schoolboy to be capped by Scotland when in 1959 he played against Ireland. Playing in this game was the former Kent all-rounder Jim Allan, and it was on his recommendation that Les Ames invited Denness for a months trial in 1961. After that he never looked back, despite failing to score in the first innings of his debut, after having unfortunately had to face Jim Laker on a turning wicket.

Denness topped the 1,000 run mark for the first time in 1963 — a feat he was to achieve on twelve occasions with a best of 1,534 runs in 1966. After winning the Man-of-the-Match award against Somerset in the 1967 Gillette Cup Final Denness, along with Brian Luckhurst, began to form the best opening partnership in the country.

The 1969 season was an important one for Mike Denness. He took over the captaincy of the county in May after Colin Cowdrey had suffered an Achilles tendon injury that was to keep him out until the last game of the season. It was also the summer that he made his England debut in the Test series against the West Indies.

When Kent won the County Championship in their centenary year, Denness stepped in efficiently to lead the side when Cowdrey was on Test match duty. It did not affect his batting as he scored 1,404 runs at 40.37.

In 1972, Mike Denness had the satisfaction of leading Kent to their first Sunday League title, in what was his first full season as captain. In 1972-73 he toured India, Pakistan and Sri Lanka as vice-captain, though his best form was shown in the next two tours, when he captained his country. In the Caribbean he helped in some remarkable recoveries as England drew the series against a much stronger West Indies team. His batting limitations, like those of the other England players on the 1974-75 tour of Australia, were exposed by the magnificent bowling of Lillee and Thomson. In fact, Denness dropped himself for the fourth Test at Sydney in which Australia regained the Ashes. He returned for the last Test at Melbourne, scoring a brilliant 188.

In 1973 under Denness leadership, Kent won three competitions — the Benson and Hedges Cup, the John Player Sunday League and the end of season Fenner Trophy. The following season he was heavily involved in Test cricket and so for the first time failed to score 1,000 runs. He returned to his prolific ways in 1975 and the following season led Kent to the Benson and Hedges Cup and John Player League title again before resigning the captaincy.

For Kent, Denness scored 17,047 runs at 32.90 and under his captaincy, the hop county won the Sunday League three times, the Benson and Hedges Cup twice and the Gillette Cup once. It was a blow to Kent when, in 1977, this outwardly tough but inwardly sensitive Scotsman left to move to Essex.

DERBYSHIRE

Founded in 1870, Derbyshires solitary Championship title came in 1936. The county also won the inaugural Nat West Trophy tournament in 1981, the Sunday League in 1990 and the Benson and Hedges Cup in 1993.

In 1938, Kents match against Derbyshire on the Bat and Ball ground was certainly one to remember. Kent won by ten wickets with the spin twins, Tich Freeman and Doug Wright, claiming 17 of the 20 wickets to fall. Freeman finished with match figures of nine for 52 and Wright eight for 80.

When Kent played Derbyshire in 1951, Fred Ridgway became the first bowler in the countys side since 1862 to take four wickets in four balls. The visitors in the shape of Donald Carr and Revill had put on 159 on an easy paced Folkestone wicket when Ridgway took the new ball. At first he did not seem eager to take it but after bowling Revill with the first ball of his second over he had Kelly caught by Arthur Fagg at first slip. The hat-trick ball saw Harold Rhodes caught by Cowdrey and the fourth saw Godfrey Evans take a splendid catch to dismiss his namesake in the Derbyshire side.

DILLEY, GRAHAM

On leaving school, Graham Dilley took a job as a diamond setter in Hatton Garden, but soon gave this up when he was offered the chance to play for the Kent 2nd XI in midweek games. During the winter months he would build up his strength for the coming summer by carrying huge sheets of plasterboard for his uncles partitioning firm. He would play for Kent 2nds in midweek and his club side, Dartford, at the weekends.

He made his first-class debut against Cambridge University in 1977 and in the following summer he played in his first County Championship game, impressing straightaway with five for 32 in Middlesexs second innings. At the end of the 1978 season, he gained early international honour when he played for England against the West Indies in the

Agatha Christie Under 19 Test series. His early performances had been enough to convince Mike Brearley and the Test selectors that he was a worthy choice to tour Australia in the winter of 1979-80. So despite still being uncapped by Kent, he packed his bags for Down Under .

He was selected to tour Australia on the basis that he was going to gain experience, but he was selected for the first Test ahead of players like Bob Willis who was struggling for fitness and form. The following summer, when the West Indies were England s opponents, he was surprisingly overlooked until the third Test at Old Trafford, going on to take 11 wickets at 16.63 runs apiece. In 1980-81 Dilley toured the West Indies and although he only took ten wickets, he impressed with his aggression and speed.

In that magnificent match at Headingley in the 1981 Ashes series, Dilley hit 56, helping Man-of-the-Match Ian Botham to put on 117 for the eighth wicket.

Dilley performed the hat-trick for Kent on two occasions; against Surrey at the Oval in 1985 and at Chelmsford in the match against Essex a year later.

At the end of the 1986 season, Kent revealed that Dilley had refused to sign a new two-year contract but it also came to light that he had asked to be released some twelve months earlier. Dilley refused to re-sign for Kent and on becoming a free agent under TCCB rules, he left to join Worcestershire, having taken 257 wickets at 27.80 runs apiece.

He spent six seasons at New Road, helping Worcestershire win the County Championship and Sunday League crown in 1988. Unfortunately he was plagued by knee and ankle problems but the greatest irony of his enforced retirement in 1992 was brought about by a recurrence of the neck injury which cut short his tour of Pakistan in 1984.

DILLON, TED

Ted Dillon made his Kent debut in 1900 while still a pupil at Rugby School. He was described in *Wisden* as the best schoolboy batsman of the year, having also covered himself with glory for Kent by averaging 36.50 from eight innings.

Dillon then went to Oxford University, making 143 for the Dark Blues against Somerset. After being the leading batsman at Oxford in his second year there, Dillon went into business. However, he maintained his form and seldom disappointed with his batting when he returned from periods of very little practice to bolster the Kent batting.

Ted Dillon was a left-handed batsman who believed in attack, with the off-drive being his favourite stroke. He used his long reach to the best advantage, driving to the off with tremendous power and placing all his forcing shots with great skill.

It was Dillon who led Kent to their Championship successes in 1909, 1910 and 1913, leading such players as the Day brothers, Punter Humphreys, Colin Blythe, Frank Woolley, Fred Huish, Arthur Fielder and Douglas Carr. He was also a batsman capable of defending bravely when needed and more or less finished his county career by leading Kent to the 1913 Championship.

Dillon, who scored 9,415 runs at an average of 28.88, was also a Rugby Union internationalist. While playing three-quarter for his club Blackheath, he was capped against Ireland, Scotland and Wales in 1904 and Wales again in 1905.

DIXON, ALAN

Although he made his Kent debut against Essex at Clacton in 1950 at the age of sixteen, for Alan Dixon the step up to the county game was a big one. For the majority of the 1950s, he was involved in club cricket with Swanscombe and Greenhithe and later Dartford. However, by 1959, he was an established member of the Kent side.

His early promise was as a batsman but in 1960 he began to bowl both medium-pace using the seam or quickish off-breaks and at the end of the season, was awarded his county cap, ten years after his debut. After passing 1,000 runs in a season for three consecutive years, his batting form dropped off. However, his bowling had given his game a new dimension and over the next few seasons he continually took more than 100 wickets.

By 1967, Alan Dixon had been appointed vice-captain to Colin Cowdrey. It was a summer in which he had two outstanding games. In the Gillette Cup game at the Oval against Surrey, this bespectacled dual-purpose bowler destroyed the Surrey batting by taking seven for 15 and winning the Man-of-the-Match award for what is still a competition record. In the game against the Indian tourists, Dixon scored a century and took five wickets.

He was awarded a benefit in 1969, but at the end of the 1970 season, he decided to retire to go into insurance full-time. In all first-class matches he scored 9,561 runs and took 929 wickets, and though he regretted never having toured, he must have enjoyed his parting shot, hitting the last ball he faced on to the roof of the mayors tent at the St Lawrence ground for a six.

DOUBLE

The feat of scoring 1,000 runs and taking 100 wickets in a season has been performed nine times by three Kent players.

	Year	Runs	Average	Wickets	Average
Frank Woolley	1910	1,050	25.60	132	13.97
	1912	1,373	45.76	107	14.48
	1914	2,192	47.77	119	19.26
	1920	1,548	39.69	164	13.43
	1921	1,638	46.80	129	16.08
	1922	1,868	53.37	142	18.00
Les Ames	1928	1,736	36.16	114 dismissals	
	1929	1,777	40.38	116 dismissals	
Leslie Todd	1936	1,211	26.91	102	20.98

Jack Mason achieved the feat in all matches in 1901, and Woolley did so in 1919 and 1923. In 1932, Ames scored 2,482 runs and made 103 dismissals in all first-class matches - he was also the first wicket-keeper to achieve this feat.

DOVER

Probably one of the greatest achievements in the construction of a cricket ground is the Crabble at Dover where an eight-acre plateau has been carved out of the side of a hill. It was opened in 1897 and a cycle track encircled the grass and athletic meetings were staged, but probably due to its isolated position, the venture seemed doomed. In desperation, after six years, it was decided to sell the land for building development but the situation was saved by a last minute offer from Dover Corporation to buy the ground.

The earliest county game was played there on 11 July 1907, and the following year the cricket week was inaugurated. In 1935 Bill Ashdown carried his bat for 305 not out to record the highest individual score on the ground, but for really memorable cricket it is necessary to look to August 1937 and the game against Gloucestershire. With Charlie Barnett hitting 70 out of the first 90 in 35 minutes, the visitors totalled 434. For Kent, Frank Woolley made 100 in two hours in a total of 399. Gloucestershire quickly added 182, leaving Kent to make 218 in just under two hours. In some of the fastest scoring ever recorded, the score-board ceased to operate as the run rate reached 185 per hour — Kent reaching their target with just minutes to spare.

DOVEY, RAY

Ray Dovey was an off-spinner who could switch to medium-pace rather in the manner of Frank Smailes of Yorkshire. However, he lacked the touches of brilliance which occasionally raised Smailes to England class.

Dovey was a reliable county performer, often supporting the formidable but eccentric Doug Wright. His best performance for Kent came in 1950 in the match against Surrey at Blackheath. He opened the bowling with Martin and took eight for 23 in 19.2 overs. He followed this with five for 52 in the second innings. It was the first time Kent had beaten Surrey in the traditional Blackheath fixture for sixteen years. *Wisden* records that Dovey turned the ball sharply into the batsmen and many fell to leg-side catches .

He was never close to England selection but he did tour, as a replacement, with the Commonwealth XI in India in 1950-51.

Dovey, who played his first game for Kent before the Second World War, ended his first-class career in 1954, having taken 751 wickets at a cost of 27.28 runs apiece.

On retirement he coached at Sherborne and thus played for Dorset before returning to Kent to coach at Tonbridge. There he combined his cricketing duties with running the school shop, something which many school professionals have done.

DOWNTON, PAUL

In his early days at Sevenoaks School, Paul Downton was helped greatly by two people in particular. The first was John Miles, an Australian who ran a coaching school in Melbourne with Frank Tyson. The other who played a leading role was Alan Hurst, a player with Cambridge

University and Essex. He was Downtons cricket master and English tutor. At Sevenoaks, the young Downton had six seasons in a side that was unbeaten for three years.

He was only sixteen when he made his debut for the Kent 2nd XI and within a couple of years was touring the West Indies with the England Young Cricketers.

Downton made his first-class debut for Kent in 1971 against Surrey at Maidstone, marking his appearance with the brilliant stumping of Alan Butcher off Asif s

Paul Downton.

bowling. In his early years in the Kent side, Downton received great help from Kent s wicketkeepers of the past — Ames, Levett and Knott. He had by now left Sevenoaks and was studying law at Exeter University. He was also beginning to feel frustrated as Knott s deputy but his selection for the MCC winter tour to Pakistan and New Zealand eased the situation.

After a great soul-searching Downton, who had claimed 99 first-class victims, decided to join Middlesex. His loyalty to the county of his birth had to make way for his need to play first-class cricket on a regular basis rather than the need to play first-class cricket for Kent on a limited basis.

Downton kept wicket for Middlesex with great determination and made thirty appearances for his country.

DURHAM

Founded in 1882, Durham entered the County Championship in 1992. Highlights in the meetings between the two counties have been few but in 2000 Durhams first visit to Tunbridge Wells saw the northern county record their lowest-ever total, 81, against Kent. Kent won by 190 runs to remain undefeated at home in their matches against Durham. At Chester-le-Street, Ed Smith made 175, the highest Kent innings against Durham. The draw ended a sequence of eight decisive results in matches between the counties.

E

EALHAM, ALAN

After some impressive performances for Ashford, Kent offered Alan Ealham terms, but his father would not let him join the staff until he had completed his apprenticeship as a welder and panel beater. At the age of seventeen he was established in the Kent 2nd XI but it was another four years before he made his first-class debut against Somerset at Bath.

One of the best outfielders in the country, he took some memorable catches. In 1967 Kent were bidding to wrest the Championship title away from Yorkshire. Alan Ealham was fielding as a substitute in the deep at a tense moment in this important game at Canterbury. Fred Trueman hit the

Alan Ealham

ball a tremendous distance and at great height and Ealham, running at full speed round the boundary, took a brilliant one-handed catch in front of the Frank Woolley stand. The Kent crowd went wild but Trueman disputed the catch, needing several minutes of convincing that he was indeed out.

In 1973 Ealham caught Chris Balderstone in breathtaking fashion — a catch shown time and time again on television transmissions. Perhaps his proudest moment came when he was 12th man for England in the Jubilee Test against Australia at Lords. He held two catches and was complimented by all in the England ranks.

In 1978 Ealham was asked to take charge of the Kent side, a team full of talent. He had his doubts but his philosophy of always having a go if the opportunity presented itself was a wise one. He kept harmony in the side despite the outside problems and under his sensible captaincy, Kent won the Championship and the Benson and Hedges Trophy.

Ealham left the first-class scene in 1981, having scored 10,996 runs at 27.62 and held 175 catches. However, the story does not quite end there, for in 1988 he left his garage business and returned to captain the Kent 2nd XI. Alan Ealham always rose to a challenge and surely his limited-overs talents, like those of his son Mark, could have been utilised by the national side.

EALHAM, MARK

The son of former Kent captain Alan Ealham, Mark is an all-rounder who bats with the same malevolent belligerence as his father, and bowls at quickish medium-pace. He progressed through the Kent Schools network and helped Ashford win the Kent League in 1986 before making his Kent debut three years later, when he scored 45 against Lancashire at Old Trafford.

However, it was 1992 before he established himself as a regular member of the Kent side, scoring 426 runs and taking 36 wickets. The following summer Ealham finished second in the batting averages with 604 runs at 54.90 and a best score of 85 against Lancashire. In fact, he scored seven fifties in his last nine Championship innings.

Ealham scored his maiden first-class century in 1995, his innings of 121 against Nottinghamshire at Trent Bridge coming in quick-fire style. That summer he created a Sunday League record, smashing a century

Mark Ealham

against Derbyshire at Maidstone off just 44 balls. In 1996, he topped the Kent bowling averages and produced his best bowling figures of eight for 36 against Warwickshire at Edgbaston. That summer saw him make his

Kent and England player Richard Ellison delivering a ball that may well have collected one of the 475 wickets he took for his county.

Test and Limited Overs debuts for England, scoring 51 and taking four for 21 against India in his Test debut.

In 1997 Ealham not only topped the Kent batting averages with 809 runs at 57.78 but also made the highest score of his first-class career — 139 against Leicestershire at Canterbury. He also made his highest Test score of an unbeaten 53 against Australia at Edgbaston.

He played his last Test match in 1998 but has continued to be an important member of Englands one-day side. In Zimbabwe in 1999-2000 he established a new record, taking five for 15. Ealham has now appeared in 60 one-day internationals, taking 66 wickets at 30.96 runs apiece.

For Kent, the popular all-rounder has scored 5,655 runs and taken 305 wickets.

ELLISON, RICHARD

After completing his studies at Tonbridge School and Exeter University, Richard Ellison was given his chance in the Kent 1st XI in 1981 and impressed with both bat and ball. There followed another useful second half of the season in 1982 before, in the summer of 1983, he bowled consistently well in all competitions. Twice in a Benson and Hedges, and then in a Nat West Trophy game, he took three wickets in the last two overs to win the game, including a hat-trick against Essex at Chelmsford. Injuries then began to hamper his progress but nevertheless he made his England debut against West Indies at the Oval in 1984.

Ellison reached his peak in 1985 when he headed the national bowling averages with 65 wickets at 17.20 runs apiece. With that summers Ashes series all square, he was recalled for the last two Tests and inspired innings victories in both matches with some magnificent swing bowling that brought him 17 wickets at 10.88.

After spending the 1986-87 winter playing in Tasmania, he returned to Kent for the start of the 1987 season suffering from back trouble. He did not play any first-class cricket at all during the summer of 1987 but assisted by an RAF rehabilitation centre, he recovered to spearhead Kents dramatic challenge for the following seasons Championship.

Ellison continued to play for Kent until 1993, taking 475 wickets at 28.99 runs apiece during twelve years with the county; his best bowling figures being seven for 33 against Warwickshire at Tunbridge Wells in 1991.

ESSEX

Founded in 1876, Essex won the County Championship on six occasions in 1979, 1983, 1984, 1986, 1991 and 1992. Essex won the Nat West Trophy in 1985 and 1997, the Benson and Hedges Cup in 1979 and 1995 and the Sunday League Championship in 1981, 1984 and 1985.

Bill Ashdown hit Kents first treble century in 1934 when his 332 at Brentwood against Essex was made in the countys highest total of 803 for four declared. During the course of his innings he added 352 for the second wicket with Frank Woolley — another county record. Ames made an unbeaten 202 and Frank Woolley 172 as Essex replied with 408. Following-on, they lost by an innings and 192 runs.

In 1938, Arthur Fagg marked his return to first-class cricket after illness by scoring 2,322 runs and becoming the first and only player to score a double century in each innings of a match. He hit 244 and 202 not out against Essex at Colchester, his individual match aggregate of 446, the highest recorded in a first-class game in England.

In 1986, Graham Dilley performed the hat-trick against Essex in the match at Chelmsford but had to wait over an hour and twenty minutes to achieve the feat. He had taken a wicket with his last ball before lunch which was extended to 84 minutes because of rain. Then he took two wickets with his first two deliveries after lunch to register a hat-trick.

EVANS, GODFREY

Godfrey Evans was taken onto the Kent staff at the age of sixteen, as a hard-hitting batsman who could also keep wicket. In 1937 his interest in boxing led him to obtain a professional licence. He had three fights as a welterweight, winning the first two on knockouts and the third on points. He broke his nose in his third fight and was given an ultimatum by the Kent Committee, boxing or cricket.

He had just made his Kent debut against Derbyshire in 1939 when along came the war. When cricket resumed in 1946, he soon established himself as a wicketkeeper in the highest Kentish traditions so it was no surprise when he was selected to go to Australia at the end of the season as understudy to Paul Gibb. After the first Test, Evans took over and went on to play in 91 Tests for England, claiming 219 victims — 173 caught and 46 stumped.

Evans batting in Test matches showed his ability right across the spectrum. At Adelaide in 1947 he showed that he could defend with patience and resource, supporting Denis Compton for ninety minutes without scoring a run. At Lords in 1952 he failed by only two runs to score a hundred off the Indian attack before lunch.

His best season with the bat for Kent was 1952 when, for the only time in his career, he topped the thousand run mark with 1,241 at 28.86.

Like so many of the cricketing greats, he thrived on the big occasion. It is probably fair to say that he was normally a better wicketkeeper for his country than for his county. Having said that, if he was just half as good for Kent as he was for England, then he would still have been the best on the county circuit.

In terms of Test cricket, there are well documented instances of his heroics behind the wickets. In 1948 at Trent Bridge, Barnes edged Jim Laker on to Evans right foot. It lobbed in the air and behind him. Evans launched himself to bring off an unbelievable catch. In 1950 at Brisbane, Loxton edged Freddie Brown to Evans but he could not hold it. The ball rebounded back towards the bowler but Evans had not finished. He dived full length down the wicket and got his glove under the ball before it hit the ground.

For Kent Evans scored 9,325 runs and claimed 554 victims. Whether he was batting or keeping wicket, there was never a dull moment when Godfrey Evans was around.

F

FAGG, ARTHUR

Arthur Fagg s cricket was born of his own enthusiasm. He would play in the local recreation ground and park and at the weekends would help Joe Murrin on the St Lawrence ground. Joe took a keen interest in young Arthur and arranged for him to have a trial. He was initially unsuccessful, but later in the season the Club and Ground team were a player short and Arthur was called into the side. Batting at No.7 he scored over 50 and earned himself a three-month trial for the following year.

Fagg made his county debut against Warwickshire in 1932. Within two years he had scored the first of 55 hundreds for the county and passed 1,000 runs for the season. In the mid 1930s, Herbert Sutcliffe, the Yorkshire batsman, was dropping out of Test cricket and England were looking for a new opening partnership. Fagg and Hutton were thought of as obvious candidates with Fagg, a year older than Hutton, considered the best of the two.

Fagg made his Test debut against India in 1936, playing in two Tests. His highest score was only 39. He fared better in the Championship, scoring 1,858 runs with a top score of 257 against Hampshire at Southampton. He toured Australia with MCC in 1936-37, but after playing in the first two Tests he contracted rheumatic fever and was invalided home. The fever affected his heart and he played no more cricket until 1938.

The summer of 1938 was a good one for Fagg. He scored 2,456 runs including nine centuries. One feat that season that is likely to remain unique was his performance in the match against Essex at Colchester when he scored 244 and 202 not out.

Fagg did not return to the post-war game until 1947 after which he scored plenty of runs for Kent. After scoring 203 against Middlesex at Dover in 1948, he saved his other scores of over 200 for the Nottinghamshire attack. He hit 221 in 1951 and 269 not out in 1953, both at Trent Bridge. Fagg played his last game for Kent in 1957, having scored 26,072 runs at an average of 36.06. A man of principles, he was later appointed to the first-class umpires list.

FAIRSERVICE, WILLIAM

William Fairservice was a professional off-break bowler, his first victim in first-class cricket being no less a player than W G Grace, whom he bowled twice in a match with the MCC at Lords.

However, in the main, up to the outbreak of war in 1914, Fairservice was the spare man of the Kent side. Even when he did get a game, he rarely got a chance to bowl on a turning wicket, with Charlie Blythe and Frank Woolley gaining preference. Kent must have been a happy county in those days, with reserves like Fairservice in the wings. There is no doubt that in different circumstances he would have been an even greater bowler.

After the war he commanded a regular place in the Kent line-up. In 1920 he reached the target of 100 wickets for the first time, finishing with 111 wickets in the Championship at a cost of 17.46 runs each. In the match with Surrey at Blackheath, he showed what he could do when conditions were in his favour. He had match figures of ten for 58, including dismissing Jack Hobbs in both innings.

Altogether Fairservice took 853 wickets at a cost of 22.59 runs apiece but left Kent at the end of the 1921 season to play Minor Counties cricket for Northumberland. He followed this with three coaching jobs at Tonbridge, Malvern and Lancing before spending a few years as licensee of the White Horse at Bridge.

After the Second World War he became scorer to the Kent 2nd XI, a position he held until he retired at the age of 77. When over 80 years old, he still assisted his son, who played for Kent and was sports master of Kings School, Canterbury, by bowling in the nets.

FASTEST HUNDRED

No records were kept of the times it took Kents early players to compile their centuries but one of the fastest must have been Frank Woolleys 63 minutes against Northamptonshire at Dover in 1934. The performance not surprisingly won him the Lawrence Trophy for that seasons fastest century.

FATHER AND SON

There have been a number of father and son combinations playing for Kent. William Fairservice (1902-1921) who captured 853 wickets at 22.59, appeared in more than 300 matches for the county. His son, Colin (1929-1930), who was sports master at Kings School, Canterbury, managed just 1,338 runs including a century

Christopher Collins played for Kent in the early 1880s and his son, George (1911-1928), was a more than useful all-rounder, scoring 6,237 runs and taking 378 wickets.

Sir Colin Cowdrey scored 23,779 first-class runs for Kent with a highest score of 250 against Essex at Blackheath in 1959. He made 114 Test appearances for England, playing his last game for his country in 1975. He passed 1,000 runs for a season on 27 occasions, a feat bettered only by W G Grace and Frank Woolley with 28. His sons, Chris and Graham, both played for Kent, Chris making six Test appearances.

Alan Ealham (1966-1982) captained Kent to the County Championship and Benson and Hedges Cup in 1978 and was one of the best outfielders in the country. His son, Mark, who has made eight Test appearances for England, is better known for his performances in Limited Overs Internationals. His five for 15 against Zimbabwe at Kimberley is an English record.

FIELDER, ARTHUR

Fielders early enthusiasm for the game of cricket was fulfilled by engagements at both Canterbury and Tonbridge before he was offered a place in the Kent side as a replacement for Bill Bradley in 1903. It was a wettish summer but he performed quite well and was selected to tour Australia that autumn with Plum Warners side. However, he did not perform to his full capabilities and only played in two of the five Tests.

It was Plum Warner, himself a notable player of fast bowling, who said that he found Fielder the most difficult of all fast bowlers. Fielder made the ball run away, bowling largely on the off-stump for catches in the slip or by the wicketkeeper. He could also pitch one on middle and leg to hit the off stump and occasionally bowled one to make the ball come back.

When Kent won the County Championship in 1906, Arthur Fielder contributed greatly to their success. His great bowling was a decisive factor — he took 172 wickets at a cost of 20.55 runs apiece. This was also the year he took all ten wickets for 90 runs when representing the Players against the Gentlemen at Lords. This distinction has not been achieved by any other player before or since. Despite his magnificent performance the Gentlemen won the game by 45 runs.

In 1907 he took 159 wickets at a cost of 16.60 runs each, including what were his best bowling figures in county cricket, nine for 108 against Lancashire at Canterbury.

He went to Australia again in 1907-08, under the leadership of Nottinghamshires Arthur Jones. Fielder played in four Test matches, taking 25 wickets at 25.08 runs each. His greatest moment came in the first innings of the first Test when his six for 82 included the wickets of Armstrong, Hill, Macartney, Noble and Trumper.

He was never rated highly as a batsman. He hit his one and only century, a chanceless 112 against Worcestershire at Stourbridge in 1909, when he and Frank Woolley established a tenth wicket record stand for Kent of 235.

Fielders career, in which he took 1,150 wickets at 20.88, was brought to an abrupt end by the outbreak of the First World War. When it ended he coached at Rugby for a number of years.

FINALS

Kent have appeared in the following limited overs finals:

Year	Opponents	Competition	Result
1967	Somerset	Gillette Cup	Won by 32 runs
1971	Lancashire	Gillette Cup	Lost by 24 runs
1973	Worcestershire	Benson and Hedges Cup	Won by 39 runs
1974	Lancashire	Gillette Cup	Won by 4 wickets
1976	Worcestershire	Benson and Hedges Cup	Won by 43 runs
1977	Gloucestershire	Benson and Hedges Cup	Lost by 64 runs
1978	Derbyshire	Benson and Hedges Cup	Won by 6 wickets
1983	Somerset	Nat West Trophy	Lost by 24 runs
1984	Middlesex	Nat West Trophy	Lost by 4 wickets
1986	Middlesex	Benson and Hedges Cup	Lost by 2 runs
1992	Hampshire	Benson and Hedges Cup	Lost by 41 runs
1995	Lancashire	Benson and Hedges Cup	Lost by 35 runs
1997	Surrey	Benson and Hedges Cup	Won by 8 wickets

FLEMING, MATTHEW

Kent captain Matthew Fleming, a former public schoolboy, first appeared for the 2nd XI in 1983 but his appearances were then restricted until he came out of the Army in August 1988. Within weeks he had earned an unexpected first team call-up, playing in the Sunday League against Sussex at the Mote.

Fleming, whose great-grandfather, Charles Leslie, played for England and apparently hit an all-run seven at Lords, made his Championship debut in 1989. The following summer he was awarded his county cap and celebrated by hitting 102 against Nottinghamshire at Tunbridge Wells.

Matthew Fleming

In the next few seasons Fleming continued to score useful runs and take valuable wickets, a number of his performances winning him both Nat West and Benson and Hedges Man-of-the-Match awards. In 1997 he produced personal bests in the Championship with both bat and ball, scoring 138 against Essex at Canterbury and taking five for 51 against Nottinghamshire at Trent Bridge.

In 1997-98 he played in the first of 11 one-day internationals for England, helping his side win the Sharjah Trophy. His highest score of 34 against the West Indies and best bowling of four for 45 against India both came in this competition.

Fleming, who took over the Kent captaincy from Steve Marsh in 1999, was named in Englands provisional World Cup squad but did not make the final cut. Last summer was his benefit season and Fleming, who has scored 8,602 runs and taken 262 wickets, led Kent to the Norwich Union League title.

FOLKESTONE

The first matches staged by Kent in Folkestone were at the Sandgate Hill ground, the original home of Folkestone CC, in 1862 and 1863.

Folkestone CC, founded in 1856, were by the turn of the century seeking a new ground. They were given a piece of land barely a mile from the town centre and close to the North Downs, which was originally a part of the Earl of Radnors Broad Mead Farm.

Under the supervision of Alec Hearne, the ground was levelled and wickets prepared in readiness for the inaugural game in 1905 when a Kent Club and Ground side visited the local team. However, the initial first-class match was not staged until twenty years later — in September 1925 when the Gentlemen played the Players. Following this match, Kent played against the MCC and hence the festival began. Matches were played intermittently from 1928 and since 1961 the Folkestone week has become a regular feature in late August.

Among the most memorable performances on the ground was a forceful 295 from Les Ames in 1933 when Kent crucified the Gloucestershire bowlers to the extent of 592 for five declared, the highest score of any county that season. Two years earlier, Herbert Sutcliffe had tamed the Kent attack for 230, still the highest individual score recorded against them at Folkestone. Fred Ridgway dismissed Revell, Kelly, Rhodes and Gladwin of Derbyshire in four successive balls. Tich Freeman fiddled out Warwickshire twice in one game when he took eight for 31 followed by nine for 61 in 1932.

FOOTBALLERS

There have been a number of Kent cricketers who have been footballers of real note.

Cuthbert Burnup, who scored 9,668 runs for Kent at an average of 38.06, played most of his football for the famous Corinthians. He made one appearance for England, in the match against Scotland at Celtic Park in 1896, a game the home side won 2-1.

Wally Hardinge played for Kent for almost a quarter of a century, scoring 32,549 runs at 36.48 and capturing 370 wickets at 26.41 runs apiece. He was one of a small number of men who played internationally at both cricket and soccer. He began his career with Newcastle United before moving to Sheffield United in 1907. One of the trickiest inside-forwards in the game, he played for England against Scotland at Hampden Park in 1910, a match the English lost 2-0. In 1913, he joined Arsenal and after hanging up his boots, had a spell as manager/coach to Tottenham Hotspurs reserve team.

After the Second World War, Kent had three players who turned out for Charlton Athletic. Winger Tony Pawson, an England Amateur international joined the Addicks from Pegasus. Derek Ufton, the clubs president, appeared in 263 League games for Charlton between 1948 and 1960. The popular centre-half was captain from 1955 and in 1953 won an international cap against the Rest of Europe. From 1965 to 1968 he was manager of Plymouth Argyle. Stuart Leary joined Charlton Athletic in 1951 and won England Under-23 honours but because of his South African origins, he was overlooked at full international level. Leary, who regularly scored 20 goals a season, netted 153 goals in 376 League games before moving to Queens Park Rangers in December 1962, scoring 29 goals in 94 games for the Loftus Road club.

FORMATION

The first accepted county match was between Kent and Surrey at Dartford in 1709 and the first Canterbury week took place in 1842. In that year, during the first Canterbury week, the Beverley Club was reconstituted as the Kent Cricket Club. In 1859 a new county club was formed at Maidstone. Both clubs ran into financial difficulties and had a meeting at the Bull Inn, Rochester on 6 December 1870 at which they amalgamated and the present Kent County Cricket Club was formed with headquarters at Canterbury.

FREEMAN, 'TICH'

There are not too many cricketers instantly recognisable by their nickname but one is Alfred Percy Freeman. In his early days as a cricketer, Freeman had been on the ground staff at Leyton where his uncle was groundsman. He played in several Club and Ground matches for Essex but they decided against engaging him.

Tich , as he was to become known throughout the cricketing world, performed nobly in the Kent 2nd XI and was the leading wicket-taker in Club and Ground matches. After making his first-class debut in 1914 against Oxford University, his career was interrupted by the First World

War. In 1919 he had to start all over again but by the end of the following season he had taken his place among the best slow bowlers of the day.

Tich , who was only 5ft 2ins in height, always hurried back to the end of his run as if he could not wait to bowl the next ball. He relied mainly on a leg-break and a top-spinner which was difficult to spot — it was his most dangerous ball and provided him with many a leg-before decision. He also possessed a much slower ball, cleverly flighted, often resulting in a skied catch or a stumping. In the main, it was the left-handers who were faced with the googly, though he would bowl it to the right-handers if necessary.

In 1920 he took more than 100 wickets for the first time, a feat he was to achieve each season until his retirement in 1936. His best performance in 1920 was his nine for 87 against Sussex at Hastings — the Sussex captain declaring when the ninth wicket went down. At Canterbury in the match against Middlesex, he performed the first of his three hat-tricks.

In 1922 Tich took 194 wickets including 17 of them in the match against Sussex at Hove when his figures in the first innings were nine for 11. In the return fixture, he claimed another 12 victims to finish with 29 wickets for 138 runs in the two matches against Sussex for an unbelievable average of 4.74.

In 1922-23 Tich toured Australia and New Zealand with Archie MacLarens MCC side, taking his second hat-trick at Adelaide in the match against South Australia.

Freemans most successful summer was that of 1928 when his victims totalled 304 (including 246 in the County Championship). Some of his better performances in that seasons Championship included 13 for 168 against Northamptonshire and 12 for 199 against Hampshire. In Englands first Test match against the West Indies, Freeman took his first wicket on home soil when Learie Constantine hit the first ball he faced from Tich into the air and Larwood took a simple catch. Freeman took 22 wickets at 13.72 runs each in the three-match series.

In 1929 Tich took all ten wickets in an innings against Lancashire for 131 runs at Maidstone. He was to accomplish the feat on a further two occasions, taking ten for 53 against Essex at Southend in 1930 and ten for 79 at Old Trafford the following year when Lancashire were once again on the receiving end.

By the end of the 1931 season Tich had claimed four great records —
he had taken more than 200 wickets for the fourth successive season; he
had established a new record aggregate of 1,122 wickets in four seasons;
he had passed Colin Blythes record of 2,231 wickets for Kent; and had
become the first bowler to take all ten wickets three times in first-class
cricket.

In 1932 he took 17 for 92 in the match against Warwickshire at
Folkestone and was the leading wicket-taker in the country with 209
Championship victims. In 1934 he performed the third and final hat-trick
of his career against Surrey at Blackheath.

The end of his career was a little sad. By 1936 he could no longer stand
the strain of a full season and it was suggested that he play only in selected
matches. Freeman rejected the proposal and the Kent Committee terminated
his engagement with the county.

Tich Freeman took 3,340 wickets for Kent at an average of 17.64 —
making him the greatest wicket-taker county cricket has ever known.

G

GILLETTE CUP

Kent first reached the final of the Gillette Cup in 1967 where their opponents were Somerset. Having won the toss, Kent got away to a wonderful start and at lunch were 129 for one. Mike Denness batted brilliantly and Brian Luckhurst, having his first knock since he suffered a broken finger, scored 50. Shepherd was out soon after lunch and this was the start of Kents rapidly declining fortunes. Somerset bowled and fielded like tigers to reduce Kent to 150 for seven, and though Knott and Ealham steadied the boat, Kent could only muster 193. Somersets openers, Virgin and Robinson, put 58 on for the first wicket but soon their innings began to follow the Kent pattern and they fell short of victory by 32 runs.

Kents second appearance in a Gillette Cup final was in 1971 when another packed Lords saw a magnificent match against Lancashire. Despite John Dyes early success, trapping England opener, Barry Wood, leg-before without a run on the board, and with Clive Lloyd hitting an exhilarating 66, Lancashire reached 224 for seven in their 60 overs. Kent too, lost an England opener without a run on the board when Brian Luckhurst failed to trouble the scorers. However, with Asif Iqbal in fine form, Kent looked as though they would succeed in overtaking Lancashires total but when he had made 89, he was brilliantly caught by Jack Bond, Lancashire going on to win by 24 runs.

In 1974, Kent gained revenge over Lancashire, winning a low-scoring game by four wickets. For the first time since the competition began in 1963, rain prevented any play on the appointed Saturday. The game got under way on the Monday. In the field Kent were brilliant, admirably backing up sustained accuracy by their bowlers. Lancashire suffered a mortal blow when Clive Lloyd slipped when turning and was run out. To make 119 looked easy for Kent and it seemed that it was at 52 for one. However, at 53 for four it was a different kettle of fish but Alan Knott put his head down and saw Kent safely home by four wickets.

In 1981, the competitions sponsors changed to the Nat West and two years later, Kent played Somerset. The final was unique in that it was the first 60-overs final to be contested in 50 overs as some thirty minutes were lost at the start of play. It was a fine game of cricket with the advantage swaying to and fro. Somerset were restricted to 193 for nine with Graham Dilley taking four for 29. Chris Tavare looked to be well in control for Kent until Vic Marks moved in with three vital wickets, leaving Somerset the victors by 24 runs.

Kents last appearance in the final came the following year, 1984, when their opponents were Middlesex. It was a day of gritty cricket with Chris Cowdrey top-scoring for Kent in their total of 232 for six. With Clive Radley chipping runs, Middlesex were always in with a shout but it needed John Emburey to hit a boundary off the last ball of the game. Had he missed it instead of cracking it to the boundary, then Chris Tavare would have lifted the cup rather than tasted defeat in the competition for a second successive year.

Kents Gillette Cup/Nat West Trophy records include:

Highest Innings Total	384 for 6 v Berkshire at Finchampstead in 1994
Lowest Innings Total	60 v Somerset at Taunton in 1979
Highest Individual Score	136* by Carl Hooper v Berkshire 1994
Best Bowling Performance	8 for 31 by Derek Underwood v Scotland in 1987
Highest Partnership	226 for the 6th wicket (N J Llong and M V Fleming) v Cheshire in 1999.

GILLINGHAM

The county staged their first fixture at the Royal Engineers, sometimes known as the Garrison ground, in Gillingham in 1937 when Kent scored 512 for three in their first innings to defeat Worcestershire by seven wickets. Les Ames top-scored in that match with 201 not out, and that remains the highest score by a Kent player on this ground.

Bowlers, too, have on occasions produced excellent figures. In 1959 Fred Ridgway and Dave Halfyard with five for 11 and five for 21 respectively, bowled out Leicestershire for just 39.

GLAMORGAN

Glamorgan, founded in 1888, have won the County Championship on three occasions — in 1948, 1969 and 1997. The county also won the Sunday League in 1993.

During the summer of 1936, when Leslie Todd did the cricketers double, scoring 1,211 runs and taking 102 wickets, he was often the despair of his captain, Percy Chapman. In the match against Glamorgan at Folkestone, Todd displayed the infuriating side of his nature. Kent needed some quick runs but Todd took two-and-a-half hours compiling his 50. Chapman sent in Levett with a message. Tell Todd hes boring me. If he doesn t get a hundred, he s dropped for the next match. Levett was soon dismissed and, though Chapman, Lewis and Watt all made a few runs, it was left to Tich Freeman to stay with Todd. In a stubborn last wicket stand, Todd, who was on 69 when Freeman arrived at the crease, was last man out for 113.

GLOUCESTERSHIRE

Gloucestershire, founded in 1871, won the unofficial County Championship in 1874, 1876 and 1877 and were joint champions in 1873. Since 1930 the county has finished second in the Championship on six occasions. Gloucestershire have had four one-day successes, winning the Gillette Cup in 1973, the Benson and Hedges Cup in 1977 and 1999 and the Nat West Trophy, also in 1999.

The highlight of a poor 1895 season was the match against Gloucestershire in which W G Grace, at the age of forty-seven, was on the field for the whole match. Opening the batting for Gloucestershire, he made 257, being the last man out. He then made an unbeaten 73 as Gloucestershire made 106 in their second innings to win the match by nine wickets.

In 1897, having only left school earlier that season, Samuel Day became the first player in the countys history to score a century on his debut. He scored 101 not out in the second innings of the match against Gloucestershire at Cheltenham.

There was some quick scoring in the match against Gloucestershire at Catford in 1909 when Kent totalled 593 in just four-and-a-half hours.

Edward Humphreys (208) and James Seymour (86) added 224 in 100 minutes for the second wicket and when Hutchings (100) joined Humphreys, 102 was added for the third wicket in just 35 minutes.

When Kent won the County Championship the following summer, the Gloucestershire attack was annihilated for a second successive season. Kent scored 607 for six in five hours with Humphreys (162) Mason (121 not out) and Seymour (90) the leading run getters.

One of Kents most memorable victories came against Gloucestershire at Dover in 1937. The home side scored 219 for the loss of just two wickets with 19 minutes to spare — obtaining the runs in just 71 minutes, averaging nine plus runs per over. During the course of the game, the Kent fans were so caught up in the excitement that they ringed the boundary to make sure the ball was returned as quickly as possible.

GRAVESEND

When Charles Dickens featured the All-Muggletonian Cricket Club in his *Pickwick Papers* it was generally accepted that it was a caricature of the Gravesend Cricket Club which resided, under slightly varying names, including the Bat and Ball, at this famous old ground since 1857.

In 1845 Tom Adams laid the first wicket in the grounds of a large mansion and in doing so set the scene for many of crickets historic moments. Kent played at Gravesend in 1856 in the first of their many conflicts with Sussex and the following year, in a memorable game against MCC, Edgar Willshire and Adams both scored double-centuries for Kent.

After interest in cricket faded, the ground changed ownership several times until Willoughby-Brown purchased it in 1879 and county fixtures were revived again. When Thomas, the youngest of the Willoughby-Browns, died in 1895 he left the ground in trust to be sold. At this point Lord Darnley called a meeting of prominent businessmen, the outcome of which was that the North Kent Cricket and Sports Company was created with the aim of preserving the old Bat and Ball ground.

What a host of memories this ground holds — the immortal W G , in one game, being on the field for every ball of a three-day match; Frank Woolley punishing the ball to every corner of the ground; Tich Freeman cunningly flighting to tease the batsman while the eager hands of Les Ames waited anxiously for a half-chance of stumping.

HALFYARD, DAVE

Unable to force his way into the Surrey 1st XI, Dave Halfyard joined Kent in readiness for the 1956 season and although he took wickets, he was quite expensive. The following season he took 117 County Championship wickets at 21.38 runs apiece including match figures of 13 for 94 in the match against Worcestershire at Folkestone — a performance that saw him perform his first hat-trick. Later that summer he claimed what were to be the best figures of his career, nine for 39 against Glamorgan at Neath.

Dave Halfyard was a super stock bowler, a captains dream. He liked nothing better than bowling, having the perfect build for hours of toil. In 1958, on a wet wicket at Hastings, he took eight for 49 to help shoot out Sussex and in the next match, against Leicestershire, performed the second hat-trick of his career. The following summer he had 15 wickets in the match against Worcestershire at Maidstone including nine for 61 in the second innings.

Halfyard, one of the mainstays of the Kent bowling attack, took over 100 wickets in five consecutive seasons with a best of 135 at 19.91 runs each in 1958.

In August 1962, Dave Halfyard was injured in a car crash. He suffered a broken right leg and lacerations to the face and missed the whole of the following season. After playing in just two games in 1964 he was thanked for his services, given a testimonial and allowed to leave. Halfyard ended his Kent career with 769 wickets at a cost of 24.47 runs each.

In 1962 he joined the first-class umpires list but all the time keeping himself fit in the hope of returning to county cricket. In 1968 he joined Nottinghamshire, becoming a regular and valuable member of the Trent Bridge side. He later played for Cornwall, turning in some memorable performances, but for Kent he was a player of great determination, liking nothing better than when he was bowling.

HAMPSHIRE

Founded in 1863, Hampshire have twice won the County Championship, first under the enthusiastic captaincy of Colin Ingleby-Mackenzie in 1961 and again in 1973, when their captain was Richard Gilliat. The county have won the Sunday League on three occasions in 1975, 1978 and 1986; the Benson and Hedges Cup in 1988 and 1992, and the Nat West Trophy in 1991.

In Kents match against Hampshire at Canterbury in 1923, Jack Bryans last season, the Kent batsman made 236 not out in a total of 345. One of his drives sent the ball into the pavilion where it became so firmly embedded in the glass of the old Canterbury picture that a new ball had to be obtained.

HARDINGE, WALLY

Wally Hardinge made his Kent debut in 1902 and went on to play for Kent for almost a quarter of a century, although it was 1908 before he really made his mark. In that season, he scored 1,341 runs at 33.52, with his best performance being at Leyton in the match against Essex, when he scored 153 and 126. He was to perform this feat on a further three occasions.

Hardinge was one of a small number of men who played internationally at both cricket and soccer. His Test debut came much later but in 1910 he played soccer against Scotland. At that time he was a centre-forward with Sheffield United but later moved to Arsenal where he ended his football career.

During the 1911 season, in the match against Hampshire, he scored 175 and 109. Against Essex at Tonbridge he carried his bat for 123 out of Kents total of 203. Also that summer, he made his debut for the Gentlemen against the Players. Hardinges best season before the war was 1913 when he scored 2,018 runs at 42.93, scoring four centuries in successive innings.

After the war, Hardinge proved invaluable as a slow left-hand bowler, capable of breaking stubborn partnerships. Perhaps for other counties he would have been a regular bowler, but he still took 370 wickets for Kent.

In 1920 he made an outstanding start to the season. He made his highest score of 127 at the Oval for the Gentlemen against the Players, and at Blackheath against Surrey, he scored 207 and 102 not out. He also carried his bat for 118 out of Kents total of 196 in the match against the MCC at Lords. His one and only Test came against Australia at Headingley that summer when Jack Hobbs had to withdraw on the opening day with an appendicitis.

The following season Hardinge scored 2,068 runs at 57.44 and carried his bat for 249 runs against Leicestershire and shared in a second wicket partnership of 307 with Jim Seymour against Worcestershire at Kidderminster. In 1926 he helped to set the Kent record for the fourth wicket partnership, putting on 297 with Percy Chapman against Hampshire at Southampton. It was the season in which he scored 2,234 runs at an average of 47.53.

In 1928, Hardinge hit the highest score of his career, 263 not out against Gloucestershire, following it with another double century, 205 against Warwickshire at Tunbridge Wells. Altogether that season he scored 2,446 runs at 59.65. Hardinge played his last game for the county in 1933, having scored 32,549 runs at 36.48, second only to Frank Woolley in the total number of runs scored by an individual for Kent.

HARRIS, LORD

Living at the family home, Belmont, he was soon involved in Kent cricket, being on the preliminary committee when Kent County Cricket Club was reformed in December 1870. The previous August he had made his debut for Kent against the MCC at Canterbury, but not performing to his full capabilities. At Oxford he captained the University to victory over rivals, Cambridge, and in 1874 headed the batting averages.

It took him a few years to establish himself in the Kent side and while at Oxford his appearances were few and far between. However, in 1872, he did tour Canada. That winter his father died and he succeeded to the title.

In 1875 Lord Harris was appointed Kents president, captain and honorary secretary and he more or less ruled the county club in some capacity or other for almost the next six decades. He was also heavily involved with the MCC — as a trustee for ten years, treasurer for 16 years and president in 1895.

When Lord Harris took charge, the fortunes of Kent were low but gradually his dedication encouraged the best amateurs to join him and a nucleus of professionals. It was certainly an uphill struggle, although his batting held the team together on many occasions. In his 157 matches, he top-scored in 68 innings.

Lord Harris took a team to Australia in 1878-79 where he scored more runs than his colleagues in the only representative match at Melbourne, which was lost. He possessed great courage. In the match at Sydney, an angry mob rushed on to the field protesting at an umpiring decision. Harris moved forward to shield one of the umpires and was hit by a stick for his trouble. Following this episode, there was something of a crisis in Anglo-Australian cricketing relations. However, it was Lord Harris who put an end to this unrest by inviting the Australians to tour England. He captained the English side to victory in what was the very first Test match held at home.

In 1882 he hit the highest score of his first-class career — 176 against Sussex at Gravesend.

Lord Harris held two government posts before becoming Governor of Bombay. He did much to popularise the game on the sub-continent and in fact organised the first English tour to India. He fought in the Boer War with the Imperial Yeomanry and was an important figure in the City of London. It would be hard to find a more representative figure in the heyday of the Empire than Lord Harris. He was a stickler for principles. When referring to the laws of the game, he insisted that Laws were made to be kept, rules made to be broken . It was this strict attitude to the laws that made him a fierce opponent of any opposing bowler who was suspected of throwing. Lancashire s Crosland and Nash were just two suspected and so Lord Harris ordered the Kent committee to cancel all fixtures against the red rose county until both bowlers were no longer in the side.

Lord Harris lived for cricket and played his last match at the age of seventy-nine. He was a formidable autocrat, fair-minded and not used to having his authority questioned, but he was sympathetic to those whose views he held in respect.

HAT-TRICKS

John Wells feat of four wickets in four balls against Sussex in 1862 was the earliest recorded in first-class cricket. Dean Headley s three hat-tricks in the same season (1996) equalled the world record. Doug Wright also took a hat-trick for the MCC against Border at East London during the

1938-39 tour and his total of seven hat-tricks is the present world record. The following players have all performed the feat for Kent:

Year	Bowler	Opponents	Venue
1862	John Wells (4 in 4)	Sussex	Hove
1875	George Hearne	Lancashire	Old Trafford
1878	William Pearce	Derbyshire	Derby
1890	Fred Martin	Surrey	The Oval
1891	William Best	Somerset	Taunton
1894	Walter Hearne	Lancashire	Tonbridge
1899	Bill Bradley	Essex	Leyton
1899	Bill Bradley	Yorkshire	Tonbridge
1900	Bill Bradley	Somerset	Blackheath
1900	Alec Hearne	Gloucestershire	Clifton
1910	Colin Blythe	Surrey	Blackheath
1910	Colin Blythe	Derbyshire	Gravesend
1919	Frank Woolley	Surrey	Blackheath
1920	Tich Freeman	Middlesex	Canterbury
1925	Albert Wright	Warwickshire	Tunbridge Wells
1933	Tich Freeman	Gloucestershire	Folkestone
1934	Tich Freeman	Surrey	Blackheath
1937	Doug Wright	Worcestershire	Worcester
1937	Doug Wright	Nottinghamshire	Trent Bridge
1938	Doug Wright	Gloucestershire	Gillingham
1939	Doug Wright	Gloucestershire	Bristol
1939	Charles Lewis	Nottinghamshire	Trent Bridge
1947	Doug Wright	Sussex	Hastings
1948	Doug Wright	Hampshire	Canterbury
1951	Fred Ridgway (4 in 4)	Derbyshire	Folkestone
1957	Dave Halfyard	Worcestershire	Folkestone
1958	Dave Halfyard	Leicestershire	Gillingham
1958	Fred Ridgway	Oxford University	The Parks
1964	David Sayer	Glamorgan	Maidstone
1977	Derek Underwood	Sussex	Hove
1985	Graham Dilley	Surrey	The Oval
1986	Graham Dilley	Essex	Chelmsford
1987	Kevin Jarvis	Middlesex	Lords
1996	Dean Headley	Derbyshire	Derby
1996	Dean Headley	Worcestershire	Canterbury
1996	Dean Headley	Hampshire	Canterbury
1996	Martin McCague	Hampshire	Canterbury

HEADLEY, DEAN

Dean Headley s father Ron, and grandfather George, played for the West Indies and when he made his England Test debut in 1997 it was the only instance of three such members of one family all playing Test cricket.

Headley began his first-class career with Middlesex in 1991 after playing Minor Counties cricket for Staffordshire. Two years later, he joined Kent in somewhat controversial circumstances that led to a brief ban and a fine after the player was deemed to have approached Kent while still under contract to Middlesex.

With Middlesex, Headley took five for 46 on his Championship debut including the wicket of Ashley Metcalfe with his very first ball. He achieved worldwide distinction in the summer of 1996 by claiming three hat-tricks against Derbyshire, Worcestershire and Hampshire. In the match against Derbyshire, Headley recorded his best-ever bowling figures, taking eight for 98 and eleven for 165 in the match. It was performances like this that led to him making his Test debut the following summer.

Sadly, his England career was blighted by a series of unfortunate injuries but nevertheless it was impressive and in fifteen Tests he took 60 wickets at an average of 27.85. Without doubt, the highlight of his international career was the Melbourne Test in 1998-99 when his astonishing spell of five wickets for 9 runs turned the game and earned England the narrowest of victories. Headley was one of the England players given a contract by the ECB, despite having to return home early from the 1999-2000 tour of South Africa after he had bowled only a few deliveries in one game.

Headley never played again. He lost a long fight to overcome a serious spinal injury and was forced to retire at the age of thirty-one, having taken 285 wickets for Kent at an average of 28.53.

HEARNE, ALEC

Although born in Ealing, Alec Hearne qualified for Kent as his father, Old George Hearne , was groundsman at Catford Bridge where Kent played many of their home games in 1875.

In his early years with the county, Hearne was a constant thorn in the side of Yorkshire and in 1885 at Bramall Lane, he had match figures of thirteen for 48 including eight for 35 in the second innings. In 1888 he performed the hat-trick when representing MCC against Yorkshire at Lords. His second hat-trick was against Gloucestershire at Clifton in 1900.

It was around this time that he switched from bowling leg-breaks to off-breaks because the strain on his elbow was beginning to take its toll. However, he was still bowling with considerable success and in 1902 had four for nought against Somerset at Taunton, five for 13 against Warwickshire at Maidstone, five for 15 against Hampshire at Tonbridge and eight for 36 against Middlesex at Lords.

The following year he produced his career-best figures, taking eight for 15 against Gloucestershire at Tonbridge. Still his greatest hope was to become a good batsman. He had started as a No.10 but worked so hard at this side of his game that for quite a few years he was Kents opening batsman.

At representative level, Hearne scored 120 and took 17 wickets in the match when playing for the South against the Australians at the Oval in 1893. Six years later at the Crystal Palace he made the highest score of his first-class career, 168 for W G Graces XI against the Australians.

In 1891-92 he toured South Africa with W W Reads team and made his only Test appearance at Cape Town. In this match his brother, George, and cousin, John Thomas, played for England and his other brother, Frank, played for South Africa.

Hearne continued to play for Kent until 1906, his last innings being an undefeated 154 against Worcestershire.

On his retirement, Hearne, who had scored 13,598 runs and taken 1,018 wickets, coached at the Tonbridge Nursery. In 1925 he replaced his cousin, Walter, as the county scorer and, in spite of being crippled by rheumatism, he kept the position until the outbreak of the Second World War.

HEARNE, GEORGE

George Hearne like his younger brother, Alec, gained his qualification for Kent through his father being in charge of the ground at Catford Bridge where Kent played all their home games in the summer of 1875.

In the main George Hearne was a bowler, left-hand, round arm and fast-medium in pace. In his first season in the Kent side, he took eight for 46 against Lancashire at Old Trafford including the hat-trick. In 1877, he became the first man to take more than 100 wickets for Kent in a season, finishing with 105 at 11.76 runs apiece. Over the next couple of seasons, Hearne produced some outstanding bowling feats. Hampshire suffered twice at his hands as he took four for 9 at Winchester and had match figures of thirteen for 75 at Southampton. He took fourteen for 130 against Derbyshire and eight for 53 against Lancashire at Canterbury. At Lords he took fourteen for 45 against the MCC. In 1877 and 1888 his efforts resulted in him taking 201 wickets at a cost of around 12 runs apiece. Altogether in his Kent career, he took 569 wickets at 16.50 runs each.

Like his brother, Alec, George developed into quite a capable left-handed batsman. His most successful season was 1886 when, in all first-class matches, he scored 1,125 runs including his highest score of 126 against Middlesex at Gravesend.

Hearnes one and only Test appearance came in the same match at Cape Town in which his brother, Alec, also made his only appearance. Unfortunately, George failed to score and did not get the opportunity to bowl.

HIGHEST INDIVIDUAL SCORES

The top individual scores by Kent players are as follows:

332	Bill Ashdown	v Essex at Brentwood	1934
305*	Bill Ashdown	v Derbyshire at Dover	1935
295	Les Ames	v Gloucestershire at Folkestone	1933
275*	Matthew Walker	v Somerset at Canterbury	1996
270	Frank Woolley	v Middlesex at Canterbury	1923
269*	Arthur Fagg	v Nottinghamshire at Trent Bridge	1953
263*	Wally Hardinge	v Gloucestershire at Gloucester	1928
260	Percy Chapman	v Lancashire at Maidstone	1927
257	Arthur Fagg	v Hampshire at Southampton	1936
257	Mark Benson	v Hampshire at Southampton	1991

HIGHEST INNINGS

The highest individual Kent scorer in first-class cricket is Bill Ashdown with 332 against Essex at Brentwood in 1934. Ashdown also hit 305 not out against Derbyshire at Dover the following summer and remains the only Kent player to have made triple centuries.

In the match against Essex, Kents total of 803 for four was made in a little over seven hours. Ashdown and Fagg put on 70 for the first wicket before Fagg departed and in walked Frank Woolley. He stayed just over three hours, making 172. Les Ames took strike and went on to make an unbeaten 202. The score at the close of play on that first day was 623 for two. While all this was going on, Bill Ashdown had unselfishly accumulated 300 runs in the day, averaging 50 runs an hour off his own bat. He was eventually out for 332, as Kent won the game by an innings and 192 runs.

HIGHEST TEAM SCORES

Kents highest score is 803 for four declared against Essex at Brentwood in June 1934. Bill Ashdown hit 332, the highest individual innings for Kent, and he was well supported by Les Ames, 202 not out, and Frank Woolley 172.

Australia made the highest score against Kent in the summer of 1921 when they totalled 676.

HONOURS

County Champions	1906	1909	1910	1913	1970	1977(joint)
	1978					
Runners-Up	1888	1908	1911	1919	1928	
	1967	1968	1972	1988	1992	1997
Gillette Cup/Nat West Trophy	1967	1974				
Finalists	1971	1983	1984			
Sunday League Champions	1972	1973	1976	1995		
Runners-Up	1970	1979	1993	1997		
Benson and Hedges Cup	1973	1976	1978			
Finalists	1977	1986	1992	1995	1997	

HOOPER, CARL

West Indian Test all-rounder, Carl Hooper, joined Kent as their overseas player for the start of the 1992 season, a campaign in which he scored 1,329 runs at 47.46. Kent finished as runners-up in the Championship and finalists in the Benson and Hedges Cup where they went down by 41 runs to Hampshire. The following season, Hooper topped the county batting

Kent and West Indies batsman, Carl Hooper.

averages with 1,304 runs at 59.27 and a career best highest score of 236 not out against Glamorgan at Canterbury. Hooper was the leading batsman again in 1993, his tally of 1,579 at 54.44 being his highest for the county. During the course of this summer, he established a new Kent record in the Nat West Trophy with an innings of 136 not out against Berkshire at Finchampstead.

Due to the West Indies tour of England, in which he hit 127 in the final Test at the Oval, Hooper was forced to miss the 1995 season when Kent won the Sunday League. He was back with the county in 1996, scoring 1,287 runs at 47.66 but again had a season off in 1997 as the West Indies entertained India and Sri Lanka.

He returned to Kent for the summer of 1998 and, in what proved to be his last season with the county, he topped the averages with 1,215 runs at 45.00. He also captured 31 wickets and produced his best bowling figures of seven for 93 against Surrey at the Oval.

Hooper scored 6,714 runs for Kent at an average of 50.48 in his five seasons with the county, whilst at international level, the Guyanan-born all-rounder has appeared in 80 Tests, scoring 4,153 runs at 33.76 and 182 limited-overs games where he has scored 4,612 runs and taken 163 wickets.

HUBBLE, JACK

Jack Hubble made his Kent debut in 1904 and although he was a very accomplished wicketkeeper, he had to concentrate on his batting up to the war, as Fred Huish was behind the wickets.

In his first season he played against Yorkshire at Harrogate — a match declared void due to the wicket being tampered with. At the end of the first day holes had appeared in it and by the start of the second morning they had been filled in. There was a biggish crowd on the ground, so the game continued for the spectators benefit, but the result did not count towards the Championship.

As a batsman, Hubble made five centuries, his highest being 189 made in less than three hours against Sussex at Tunbridge Wells in 1911.

In 1919, Hubble replaced Fred Huish behind the wickets and although he was not in the same league, he was a most reliable county wicketkeeper. Two years later he represented the MCC against the Australians at Lords. Few MCC batsmen could stand up to the pace of Gregory and McDonald but Hubble showed his value with knocks of 42 and 25.

His best performance as a wicketkeeper came in 1923 when he claimed ten victims in the match against Gloucestershire at Cheltenham. His first-class career ended in 1929 having scored 10,229 runs and helped to dismiss 628 batsmen. Afterwards he continued to play and umpire for the MCC and run his own sports business.

HUISH, FRED

A Surrey man who played for Kent, Fred Huish learned his craft from Harry Wood, the Surrey wicketkeeper who was Kentish by birth.

Fred Huish made his first-class debut in 1895 and was one of the most able and least demonstrative wicketkeepers of his generation. A contemporary of Warwickshires Dick Lilley who was a better batsman, Huish, despite his obvious international class, never represented his country.

Huish showed his abilities, albeit in lucky fashion, in Kents match against the Australians at Canterbury in 1902. He was standing back to Bill Bradley when Australia s Duff played the ball a few yards behind the wicket and his partner set off for a run. To get the ball, Huish had to move quite a way and, realising that he would not have time to gather it before the batsman got home, he tried to kick the ball to the wicket at his end. Huish had put so much power into his kick that the ball missed the nearest set of stumps but went on and hit the wicket at the other end, Duff being run out by a yard.

Huish s skill in taking the slow bowler was a vital factor in Kents great championship years. He was among the few to assist in the taking of 100 wickets in a season, a feat he achieved on two occasions. In 1911, his total of 101 saw his greatest triumph come against Surrey at the Oval. The occasion was Herbert Strudwick s benefit match and Huish claimed ten victims, nine of them stumped. In 1913 he raised his tally of victims to 102, helping Kent win their fourth Championship title.

On becoming Kents senior professional, Huish was reputed to exercise remarkable control over his playing colleagues. The story goes that, unless he appealed, no other professional dared to ask for a catch at the wicket. Fred Huish was the first in a line of exceptional Kent wicketkeepers and claimed 1,253 victims. He died at Northiam in Sussex at the age of eighty-seven.

HUMPHREYS, EDWARD

Edward Humphreys or Punter as he became known, arrived at Tonbridge at the age of sixteen with his pads strapped around his bat ready to play in a trial game. When he came on to bowl, he delivered a no-ball and was immediately sent from the field by Lord Harris. Humphreys thought that was the end of his hopes of playing for Kent but a year later he made his first appearance for the county.

He was then a slow left-arm bowler but it was not long before he gained greater recognition as a right-hand opening batsman. In 1904 he scored 1,524 runs at 36.28, and two years later he turned in his best bowling figures of seven for 33 against Middlesex at Tonbridge.

Humphreys was a first team regular for Kent throughout the successful years of 1906 to 1913 when they won the County Championship on four occasions. In 1908 he helped Arthur Day put on 248 in what is still a Kent record for the seventh wicket in the match against Somerset at Taunton. The following year he hit the highest score of his career, 208 against Gloucestershire at Catford. In 1910 he totalled 1,618 runs at 36.77 including another double hundred, 200 not out against Lancashire at Tunbridge Wells.

In 1912 he represented the Players at Lords and was not far from being selected for the full England side. In 1912-13 he went to the West Indies as a member of the MCC team and enjoyed a successful tour, scoring 461 runs at 40.07 and taking 40 wickets at a cost of 16.57 runs apiece.

Throughout his career, which spanned the years from 1899 to 1920, Humphreys scored 15,308 runs and took 306 wickets. He also earned recognition for his superb fielding at either mid-on or short leg.

After finishing first-class cricket, he became coach at Uppingham School where he was instrumental in the development of Percy Chapman and Gerry Chalk. He later returned to Kent as chief coach, seeing the rise of fellow Kent greats as Godfrey Evans, Arthur Fagg and Doug Wright. He was still coaching at the Nursery to within a year of his death in November 1949.

HUNDRED WICKETS

Twenty Kent players have performed the feat of taking 100 or more wickets for the county in a season with Tich Freeman having done so on seventeen occasions. The first player to do so was George Hearne in 1877 when he took 105 wickets at 11.76 runs apiece.

The most wickets taken in a season is 262 — by Tich Freeman in 1933. The last player to take a hundred wickets for the county was Derek Underwood in 1983 when he took 106 at 19.28 runs each.

HUTCHINGS, KENNETH

A true man of Kent, Kenneth Hutchings had a great career at Tonbridge, being in the School XI for five years, heading the batting averages for the last three seasons. He hit 205 against West Kent and took hundreds off the Band of Brothers, Old Cliftonians and Free Foresters twice.

He made his Kent debut in 1902, but it was not until the following summer that he first gave evidence of his ability in county cricket, with 106 against Somerset at Taunton. He then produced little until 1906, a year that will never be forgotten in Kent cricket. He was the most brilliant of batsmen that season, making his runs quickly and attractively. He did not make his first appearance until mid-June, but he started with 125 and 97 not out against Middlesex. In the next game, against County Champions Yorkshire, at Sheffield, he made 131. His next hundred was his highest score of 176 made in three hours against Lancashire at Canterbury. His final century that season came against Hampshire at Bournemouth, Hutchings ending the summer with 1,454 runs at an average of 60.68.

In 1907 he hit another four centuries, two of them in the match against Worcestershire, where he had just returned to the side following an injury. At the end of the season he went off with A O Jones s team to tour Australia but his only decent score of 126 came at Melbourne — in the only Test England won.

Over the next few seasons, Hutchings continued to score prolifically for Kent. He was a fierce driver and certainly did not believe in hanging around at the wicket. He was also equally good off the back foot, being able to play the ball at the last moment. He dropped out of the Kent side after the 1912 season, having scored 7,977 runs at 35.29.

Two years into the First World War, Lieutenant Kenneth Hutchings of the 4th Battalion The Kings Liverpool Regiment was killed in battle. He was just two months short of his thirty-fourth birthday.

J

IGGLESDEN, ALAN

Alan Igglesden originally plied his trade with Holmesdale in the Kent League before joining Kent. He showed encouraging form during 1986, his first season in the Kent team, until a side muscle injury ended his summer earlier than expected. In fact, Igglesdens entire career with the county was to be plagued by injury and he never actually played a full season.

Alan Igglesden in action.

During his first few years with Kent, Alan Igglesden showed himself to be one of the most promising English-qualified fast bowlers on the county circuit. He showed his immense potential in 1988 when, on his return to the side towards the end of the campaign, he captured wickets at a remarkable strike rate to bolster the club s challenge for the Championship.

After four years playing and coaching in South Africa where, early in 1989, he had an operation on a troublesome knee, he toured Zimbabwe with the England A side having made his full Test debut against Australia at the Oval in the summer of 1989.

It was when playing in South Africa for Boland in the winter of 1992-93 that Igglesden produced his best bowling figures in first-class cricket, taking seven for 28 against Griqualand West at Kimberley. For Kent, his best figures were six for 34 against Surrey at Canterbury in 1988.

Igglesden, who went on to take 503 first-class wickets at 26.81 runs apiece, left the county at the end of the 1998 season to play Minor County cricket for Berkshire.

INDIA

When Kent entertained the Indian tourists at the St Lawrence ground in 1952, there was an occurrence which one hopes was a one-off. Indias opening batsman, Polly Umrigar, had hammered the Kent bowling to all corners of the ground, eventually falling for a magnificent 204. During the course of his innings, Fred Ridgway lost his control and after running in to bowl, deliberately threw the ball at Umrigar. He was not no-balled because umpire Alec Skelding at square-leg was not paying attention.

Colin Cowdrey, who was born in India, scored his maiden century for the county against the tourists in this same match. Co-incidentally, his father was top scorer for the Europeans against the 1926-27 touring team in India.

IQBAL, ASIF

Asif was seventeen when he played for Hyderabad in the Ranji Trophy and in 1961, when Pakistan toured India, he represented the South Zone against them. Also that year he played against Ted Dexters MCC side. Around this time, most of his family, who were Muslims, had emigrated to Pakistan and Asif later joined them.

In 1963 the Pakistan Eaglets, comprising of promising youngsters and a fair number of Test players, left for a short tour of England. His performances on this tour led to him winning his first Test cap for Pakistan against Australia at Karachi where he batted at No.10 in the first innings, scoring 41. On his first major tour to Australia in 1965, he was the leading wicket-taker in Test matches and headed the first-class bowling averages for the tour.

At the beginning of 1967, Asif was made captain of the side to face an

MCC Under-25 team. The MCC manager was Les Ames, and he at once recognised Asif s leadership qualities. In their second encounter Asif hit his maiden first-class hundred — an innings that guaranteed him making the trip to England.

During the Oval Test, Asif hit 146 in three hours, the highest score by a No.9 in a Test match. In his first appearance against Kent, Colin Cowdrey sounded him out about him joining the hop county. Asif, pictured right, joined Kent in 1968, bringing with him an uninhibited brand of cricket. He was a batsman of quality, a bowler who could cut or swing the ball and a fielder with superb reflexes. He was at the peak of his powers in 1970, scoring 1,379 runs at 39.40, and the following summer he hit 91, an innings that nearly brought Kent victory against Lancashire in the Gillette Cup Final.

On six occasions Asif scored a thousand or more runs for Kent in the County Championship and he captained the side in 1977 and 1981-82 with great inspiration.

At Test level, he hit three centuries in four different series during 1976-77. Against New Zealand he scored 166, helping Javed Miandad set a fifth wicket record of 281. In Australia he averaged 78.25, scoring 313 runs, including centuries at Adelaide (152 not out) and Sydney (120), following it with 135 against the West Indies at Kingston, Jamaica. In all, he played in 58 Tests for Pakistan, scoring 3,575 runs at 38.85 including eleven centuries. It was Asif who used the Packer affair in a positive way to get better money for all Pakistan s cricketers. He was a constant and thrilling match-winner for both Kent and Pakistan, and he scored 13,231 runs for the hop county at 37.06.

JOHNSON, GRAHAM

When Graham Johnson joined the Kent staff, it was primarily as an off-spin bowler, but he developed into a batsman who also bowled. He made his Kent debut in 1965 but because Underwood and the Kent seamers were bowling well, his chances were rather limited.

In 1970, however, he played a significant part in Kents Championship success, scoring 927 runs. He was soon being hailed as an outstanding prospect in terms of both Kent and English cricket.

When Underwood was away on Test duty, Johnson had an opportunity to bowl. He rarely ran through a side, but performed with great consistency, adding variety to an all-seam attack. He also had the knack of picking up wickets at crucial times and, as the 1970s wore on, he became an essential part of the Kent

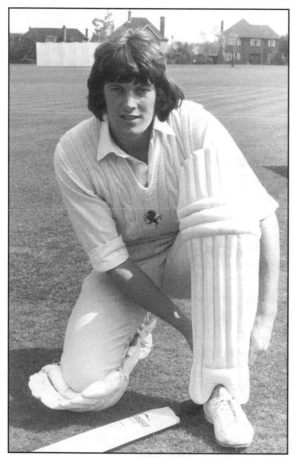

Graham Johnson – twenty years with Kent.

bowling line-up. In 1973 Johnson passed 1,000 runs in a season for the first time, scoring 1,362 runs at 33.42. He achieved this feat for three successive seasons, culminating with his 1,366 runs in 1975 being the most runs scored by a Kent player that summer.

A cartilage operation and a series of niggling injuries restricted his appearances over the next couple of seasons and when he did return to action, he found himself opening the innings at one-day level but batting at No.7 in the Championship. Many Kent supporters thought he had found his real niche in the game.

When Mike Denness departed at the end of the 1976 season, Johnson was overlooked for the captaincy. He went on to play for Kent until 1985 under various captains, his adaptability in changing circumstances serving him well.

In his twenty years with Kent, he scored 12,549 runs and took 555 wickets — but Graham Johnson was one of many good county cricketers whose statistics do not do justice to their many talents. He sacrificed his personal aims and ambitions to ensure Kent's success, always remaining as an integral part of the county side.

KNOTT, ALAN

Shortly before he turned professional, Kent suggested that Alan Knott play for Blackheath, the best side in the area. During the summers of 1961 and 1962, he played as a semi-professional with Kent. When he made his debut fot the Kent 2nd XI he did not keep wicket but played as a spinner

In 1965, a year after making his first-class debut, Knott claimed a total of

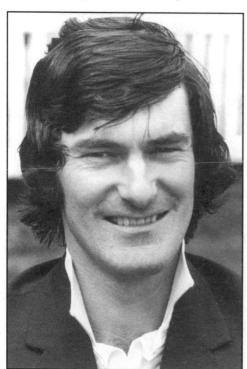

81 victims — 72 caught and nine stumped — and was elected as Young Cricketer of the Year.

He made his England debut in 1967 against Pakistan at Trent Bridge when he was just twenty- one years old and took seven catches, each one of them different. On the county scene, he claimed 85 dismissals (78 caught and 7 stumped) his highest in a season.

His best performance behind the wickets came against Leicestershire at Folkestone, where he held six catches in one innings.

At international level, Knott gained a regular place as England s wicketkeeper after his performance in the fourth Test of the West Indies tour at Georgetown. England needed to bat all day or score 308 to win the game. At 41 for five, with Boycott, Edrich, Graveney, Barrington and D Oliveira back in the pavilion, Knott joined his Kent colleague and England captain, Colin Cowdrey. The pair added 127 for the sixth wicket on a wearing pitch. Cowdrey fell for 82 but Knott was left undefeated on 69 after receiving valuable assistance from Snow, Lock, Pocock and Jones, who lasted out the final over.

In 1972 he scored a century in each innings of the match against Surrey at Blackheath, both of them unbeaten. In 1973 he was as inspiring as ever behind the stumps and in the match against Worcestershire at Dartford, he once again dismissed six batsmen in an innings.

Knott learned much of his wicket-keeping from Les Ames, Hopper Levett and Godfrey Evans. In a typical day behind the stumps he would go through his routine of calisthenics. Knottys shirt collar was always turned up to keep the sun off his neck and his sleeves rolled down to protect his elbows when he dived.

In 1977 he set a record for the most dismissals in a match. This came at Maidstone against Leicestershire when he caught nine batsmen.

After playing in the Centenary Test at Melbourne, he became one of the first recruits to Kerry Packers World Series Cricket. At the time he had played in 89 Tests, and went on to play in six further Tests, scoring 4,389 runs at 32.75 for England and helping to dismiss 269 batsmen.

Probably the finest wicketkeeper since the Second World War, Alan Knott, who retired in 1985, scored 11,339 runs for Kent and helped to dismiss 831 batsmen in his 349 matches.

L

LANCASHIRE

Founded in 1864, Lancashire have won the County Championship on seven occasions and were joint-champions in 1950. They have made their name as one-day specialists, having won the Gillette Cup/Nat West Trophy in 1970, 1971, 1972, 1975, 1990, 1996 and 1998. They won the Benson and Hedges Cup in 1984, 1990, 1995 and 1996 and the Sunday League in 1969, 1970, 1989 and 1998. In 1999 they were champions of the CGU National League Division One.

In 1885, Kent did not play their return game with Lancashire because of a dispute about the legality of delivery of two of their bowlers. Lord Harris made his view very clear before the first match between the two counties at Old Trafford, protesting against both John Crosland and George Nash. After the game, Lord Harris said in a letter to the press that he intended to advise his committee not to field a side for the return match with Lancashire, who would win by default.

In the match at Maidstone in 1927, Percy Chapman played one of his greatest innings for the county. With Kent struggling at 70 for five, he came to the wicket and, along with Geoff Legge, proceeded to add 284 in two-and-a-half hours. Legges contribution was 101 but it was Chapman with 260 (five sixes and 32 fours) who turned the game Kents way.

Tich Freeman turned in a number of remarkable bowling performances against Lancashire. In 1929 he took all ten wickets for the county for the first time with ten for 131 in 42 overs. The following year he repeated the feat with ten for 79 at Old Trafford, a ground on which he also produced his best Test figures, taking 12 for 171 against South Africa in 1929.

LEARY, STUART

Born in Cape Town, South Africa, Stuart Leary gained a big sporting reputation at school. Although he was the school cricket captain, he showed more promise as a soccer player and was persuaded by Charlton

Athletic manager Jimmy Seed to join the Addicks. Playing as a deep-lying centre-forward, he had superb control and vision, creating goals both for himself and fellow South African, Eddie Firmani. In fact, Leary s total of 153 League goals for Charlton is still a club record.

In his early days at the Valley, he mentioned to Jimmy Seed that he enjoyed playing cricket. He went to Seed s home town of Whitburn to play Durham League cricket before Kent stepped in and Leary joined the county staff in 1951. Unfortunately his development was delayed due to his commitments on the soccer field and two years National Service.

As a batsman, Leary was at his best in a crisis. His unorthodox approach to batting sometimes offended the purists and because of his reputation as a slow scorer he was once left out of a one-day match in 1969. He returned to hit three sixes in the next match and 1970 won the country s top six-hit competition. Leary topped 1,000 runs in a season on nine occasions but it must be remembered that until he gave up playing soccer in 1964, he was never available after Canterbury week.

Leary scored 16,169 runs for Kent at an average of 30.79 and made 158 — the highest score of his career — against Northamptonshire. He was also a respected leg-break and googly bowler, taking 140 wickets at 33.67 runs each. As a fielder, he was one of the best in the game, his razor-sharp reflexes bringing him 362 catches, many at short leg. In 1958 at Fenners, Leary equalled the Kent record by taking six catches in an innings in the game against Cambridge University.

He was a brilliant all-round sportsman, playing 381 first-class matches for Kent and 470 Football League matches for Charlton Athletic and Queen s Park rangers. He did gain an under-23 cap for England but was later judged ineligible due to his South African origins.

After the 1971 season he returned home to South Africa where he took up various coaching appointments. Sadly he was found dead on Table Mountain some four days after his car had been found abandoned.

LEICESTERSHIRE

For many years a Cinderella county, Leicestershire, founded in 1879, became a power to be reckoned with after the appointment of Ray Illingworth in 1969. They were the inaugural winners of the Benson and Hedges Cup in 1972 and also won it in 1975 and 1985. They won the

Sunday League in 1974 and 1977 and captured the County Championship title in 1975 and 1996 when they lost only one game.

It was in the match at Leicester in 1922 that Wally Hardinge set a new record for the county with an unbeaten 249. In a stand of 88 with Bill Ashdown, Hardinge made 80 — and four of the other runs came from byes. He was on the field throughout the match, scoring 13 not out in Kents second innings.

The following season Tich Freeman was at the crease when a ball from Geary hit his off stump and went for four byes. Although the delivery had removed the bail from its groove, it did not fall to the ground.

LEVETT, HOWARD

Hopper , as he was known, was probably second only to Les Ames as the country s best wicketkeeper in the mid 1930s.

Levett made his county debut against Worcestershire at Tunbridge Wells, having the misfortune to drop Fox early on off the bowling of Freeman, who was none too pleased. His opportunities in the first team over the next four years were restricted but after 1935, following a back injury to Ames, he began to keep wicket on a regular basis.

Hopper was among the most colourful and lovable Kent players. That he played only once for his country is a guide to the standard of wicket-keeping of his time. He was a source of encouragement to the bowlers, always urging them hard. He had days of brilliance when he was the best wicketkeeper in the land. All told, Levett dismissed 397 batsmen in his career with Kent and a further 70 in other first-class games.

Life was never dull when Hopper was playing. At Canterbury in 1938, the Australians in their second innings only needed seven to win. They sent in tail-enders and Hopper was allowed to be the first Kent bowler. When he delivered the first ball , a bread roll arrived instead of the ball. The nickname of Hopper originated from his captain, Percy Chapman — it had no connection with the Hoppers Tie Club which was founded much later on. It was a most appropriate nickname because Howard Levett grew hops for a living.

He was one of the great characters in this wonderful game of cricket. It was reported that after a night on the tiles, he remained totally motionless as the first ball of the morning and the match whistled past him for four byes. The batsman deflected the next delivery down the leg-side. Levett dived, caught it and came up triumphantly with the ball clutched firmly in his hand saying Not bad for the first ball of the day, eh?

LOWEST

Kent s lowest score of 18 was made against Sussex at Gravesend in 1867. Their lowest score in the Official County Championship is 32 against Hampshire at Southampton in 1952.

Warwickshire have made the lowest score against Kent, being all out for just 16 at Tonbridge in 1913. Both Colin Blythe and Frank Woolley had figures of five for eight as Kent ran out winners by six wickets.

LUCKHURST, BRIAN

On leaving school, Brian Luckhurst successfully passed the Naval Dockyard examination but when Kent offered him a position on the groundstaff, there was only one choice for him. Shortly afterwards he did his National Service in the Royal Artillery and he played for the Army and Combined Services as an all-rounder, but by the time he returned to Kent, he was batting in the middle order and only bowling occasionally.

Brian Luckhurst.

Although he made his Kent debut against Worcestershire in 1958, it was a good few years before he established himself as a first team regular.

Having scored more than 1,000 runs in three consecutive seasons up to 1965, he slipped easily into the role of opening batsman, usually partnered by Mike Denness. Up to that season he was still playing football in the Medway League but a broken collar bone made him realise that had the injury been more serious, it could have ended his cricket career, so the football had to go.

Luckhurst continued to score runs freely but it was not until Kents match against the Rest of the World in 1968, when he scored 113 and 100 not out, that people began to sit up and take notice of this staunch county batsman. Luckhurst scored 1,914 runs, his highest contribution in fourteen consecutive seasons of passing a thousand runs.

During Kents Championship-winning season of 1970, Luckhurst was selected to represent England against the Rest of the World. In the second Test at Trent Bridge he hit an unbeaten 113, helping England to victory even though it did take him seven hours.

His official Test career began the following winter when he played a vital part in Illingworths Ashes-winning side. He batted with a new found freedom, scoring 455 runs at 56.87, hitting hundreds at both Melbourne and Perth.

The following summer Luckhurst led the way at the top of the Kent batting averages, scoring 1,368 runs at 50.66. In 1972 he ended the season with his highest average in the County Championship — 64.85. In the following season he hit the highest score of his first-class career — 215 against Derbyshire.

Luckhursts magnificent contribution to Kent cricket, 19,096 runs at 38.00, ended when he broke his finger at Maidstone in the match against Northamptonshire. He then became captain of the 2nd XI, helping the younger players in their preparation for the step to first-class cricket. Brian Luckhurst, at one time Kents manager, is now the countys Business Development manager.

MAIDSTONE

When the loveliest county cricket grounds in England are mentioned, the Mote ground at Maidstone is always included in any short list. It dates back to the thirteenth century and within the park is the Mote House, a late eighteenth century building which is now a Cheshire Home. The cricket grounds creation coincided with the formation of the Mote CC in 1857, making it one of the oldest in the county.

Kent played their first match at the Mote in 1859 when an MCC team were the visitors. Further matches were played against Surrey and Cambridgeshire in 1861 and 1862 respectively but it was not until 1870 that Kent began to play there regularly. A cricket week was granted to the Mote in 1907, after one or two earlier experiments. Then there were two seasons when Kent did not play there at all. The week was resumed in 1910 and has been a permanent feature of Kent cricket ever since.

Although it has been the custom for many years for touring teams to play at Canterbury, the 1890 Australian side played one of their two matches against Kent at the Mote and the Philadelphian and South African sides of 1897 and 1912 respectively played Kent at the Mote.

Over the years, county cricket at the Mote has been by no means uneventful. In 1927, Percy Chapman scored 260 in three hours against a Lancashire side that included Ted McDonald — it was the highest first-class innings on the ground. In 1947, Kent scored 580 against Essex on the first day. The best bowling figures recorded are Tich Freemans ten for 131 in 42 overs against Lancashire in 1929. Dave Halfyard took nine for 61 against Worcestershire in 1959 and had a match analysis of 15 for 117.

MARRIOTT, CHARLES

When Charles Marriott made his first-class debut for Lancashire against Essex in 1919, it was the first time that he had been present at a county game.

He studied at Cambridge University, gaining a Blue in 1920 and 1921. During this latter year he was chosen for the England squad in the Old Trafford Test but was eventually left out. After his three seasons with Lancashire, he took a job at Dulwich College as master-in-charge of cricket. Thereafter he played for Kent during the summer holidays, making his debut in 1924. That summer he began his link with Tich Freeman that was to become the deadliest leg-break combination that English county cricket was ever to know.

Father Marriott, as he was popularly known, went on two tours abroad. The first was in 1924-25 when he went on Lord Tennysons trip to South Africa.

In 1933, Marriott took 54 wickets at 18.44 runs apiece. This was the season when he played in his one and only Test match against the West Indies at the Oval. That he was picked at all was a magnificent tribute to his skill as a bowler because he was an unbelievably bad batsman and was wholly unathletic in the field. His debut was sensational, his first over being a maiden to the great George Headley. He then proceeded to bewilder the West Indians as he took five for 37 in their first innings. In the second innings he had figures of six for 59 as the West Indies were beaten by an innings and 17 runs. That he only played in one Test match, despite his skill as a spinner, was very surprising.

In 1933-34 he was in the MCC squad that visited India, performing the hat-trick in the match against Madras. He played his last game for Kent in 1937 after which he went back to being a schoolmaster.

In all first-class matches for Kent, he took 463 wickets at a cost of 20.28. He had just completed a book called *The Complete Leg-Break Bowler* when he died in October 1966, a man of great charm, loved by everyone.

MARSH, STEVE

Steve Marsh spent several years in the shadows of Alan Knott before the former England wicketkeepers retirement allowed him to establish a regular place in the Kent side in 1986 — one which he held until the arrival of the much younger Paul Nixon in 2000.

During the winter of 1985-86, under the watchful eye of Bob Woolmer in Cape Town, Marsh played and coached with the Avondale club. Kent officials must have been pleased for the following summer he not only replaced Knott but his batting improved to the extent that he scored 857 runs at an average of 30.60. A bad eye injury the following summer forced him to miss half that campaign.

Marsh was extremely agile and a far better batsman than he was often given credit for, scoring 10,098 runs at 28.05 and having a top score of 142 against Sussex at Horsham in 1997.

Westminster-born Marsh, who was a great favourite with the Kent supporters, achieved distinction against Middlesex at Lords in 1991 when he established a World record by holding eight catches in an innings and then scoring a century in the same match. In that year, in which he was appointed Kents vice-captain, he also made two appearances for England A in limited overs internationals and was generally considered unlucky not to get a full England cap.

Marsh became captain of Kent in 1996, having led the side for much of the previous season when Mark Benson was forced to drop out because of a knee injury. He captained Kent for three seasons before Matthew Fleming took over in 1999.

Steve Marsh.

His safe hands, agility and consistency inspired his team mates for he helped to dismiss 749 first-class victims (688 caught and 61 stumped).

On retiring in 2000, Marsh became an executive of the commercial arm of the Professional Cricketers Association — his brief, to narrow the gap between grassroots and professional cricket.

MASON, JACK

In the summer of 1893, Jack Mason stepped out of the Winchester XI and into the Kent side, appearing in the 36 run win over the touring Australians. For the next few seasons he continued to give good all-round service and in 1897 went with Andrew Stoddart s side to Australia. He took part in all five Tests but nothing shows more clearly the strength of English cricket at that time because Mason never played in a Test in England. Often quoted as the best player never to represent England in this country, he did appear on a regular basis for the Gentlemen against the Players. In a match at Lord s, Mason was batting with W G Grace. They had put on 130 runs with W G on 78, when Mason called him for a short run. W G was run out — Mason had forgotten the great man s age and weight.

In 1898 he succeeded Frank Marchant as Kent captain. He led the county well for the next five years and would have done so for much longer had not the calls of his profession as a solicitor necessitated his resignation. Mason played on a regular basis until 1906 — from then until war broke out, he played only infrequently.

In 1899 he shared in what is still a third wicket record stand for Kent. Batting with Alec Hearne against Nottinghamshire at Trent Bridge, he helped to put on 321 runs.

Jack Mason was primarily a forward player, possessing a powerful drive and a most effective cut. Always playing with a straight bat, he went on to score 15,563 runs at an average of 33.98. As a bowler he had a model action and a high arm, making the ball run away. He bowled at a fast-medium pace, taking 769 wickets at 22.06 runs apiece. There have also been few greater slip fielders. Mason was part of a slip cordon which included Hutchings and Seymour. It has been said that after a catch had been taken, the ball would be passed from one to another so quickly that often the scorer could not tell who had caught it.

In 1938 he became President of the Kent County Cricket Club. He died in October 1958 at the age of eighty-four, one of the most popular and respected of Kent players.

MCCAGUE, MARTIN

Born in Northern Ireland but raised in Australia, he was a product of the Australian Cricket Academy in Adelaide and played eleven matches for Western Australia (1990-92) in the Sheffield Shield. He swapped the heat of Perth for the Garden of England, making his Kent debut in 1991. He played in eight Championship matches, with a best return of six for 88 against Leicestershire. His breakthrough came the following summer when his 53 wickets in 16 Championship matches included eight for 26 against Hampshire. That season McCague, pictured right, also claimed 49 victims in one-day cricket, including a hat-trick against Leicestershire — the most by a Kent player.

His reputation grew rapidly and in 1993 he made his Test debut for England against Australia at Trent Bridge. The hostility in his bowling delighted England supporters as he claimed the wickets of Taylor, Boon, Steve Waugh and May to take four for 121 from 32.3 overs.

In 1994 McCague topped the Kent bowling averages, his 54 wickets costing just 17.64 runs apiece. Included in this total were his career-best figures of nine for 86 against Derbyshire. McCague s most successful season in terms of wickets taken was 1996 when he dismissed 75 batsmen at a cost of 24.20 runs each. Sadly since then, injuries have hampered his progress, although at the time of writing he has claimed 386 victims at 25.54.

Yet to score a first-class hundred, he holds the record for Kent s fastest Sunday League half-century, his 50 coming off just 20 balls in the match against Leicestershire Foxes in August 2000.

MIDDLESEX

Founded in 1863, Middlesex won the unofficial county title in 1866 and won ten official Championships, their last being in 1993. They have also won seven one-day competitions — the Gillette Cup in 1977 and 1980, the Benson and Hedges Cup in 1983 and 1986, the Nat West Trophy in 1984 and 1988 and the Sunday League in 1992.

During Kents first County Championship-winning season of 1906, Ken Hutchings made his first team debut against Middlesex. A comparative unknown, he scored 125 and 97 not out and, along with Fred Huish, who despite suffering from lumbago and needing a runner, helped Kent survive the final few minutes and so save the game.

In the final game of the 1908 season, Kent had a dramatic win over Middlesex at Lords, when Frank Woolley took the last six wickets for eight runs in just 27 balls.

Les Ames scored his hundredth and last century in the match against Middlesex at Canterbury in 1950. The home side had been set 237 to win in two-and-a-half hours and Middlesex paceman John Warr was repeatedly hit back over his head as Ames went down the wicket to him. He finished with 131 out of 211 in two hours as Kent won with just minutes to spare.

During the 1972 Sunday League competition, Middlesex had been bowled out for 127 and Kent on 126 for six looked certain to win. They then proceeded to lose their last four wickets without scoring a run to leave Middlesex winners by one run. Kent secretary, Les Ames, had already made out the winners cheque and had to tear it up and write out another one. Yet despite this defeat, Kent went on to win the Sunday League Championship after beating Worcestershire on the final day of the season.

MOST RUNS

The following batsmen have scored the most runs for Kent:

	Runs	Average
Frank Woolley	47,868	41.77
Wally Hardinge	32,549	36.48
Les Ames	28,951	44.33
James Seymour	26,818	32.66
Arthur Fagg	26,072	36.06
Colin Cowdrey	23,779	42.01
Bill Ashdown	22,309	30.64
Bob Wilson	19,458	32.10
Leslie Todd	19,407	31.50
Brian Luckhurst	19,096	37.96

MOST WICKETS

The following bowlers have taken the most first-class wickets for Kent:

	Wickets	Average
Tich Freeman	3,340	17.64
Colin Blythe	2,210	16.67
Derek Underwood	1,951	19.21
Doug Wright	1,709	22.68
Frank Woolley	1,680	18.84
Arthur Fielder	1,150	20.88
Alec Hearne	1,018	19.96
Fred Ridgway	955	23.81
Fred Martin	947	18.16
Alan Dixon	929	26.69

NEW ZEALAND

In 1931, Frank Woolley and Les Ames recorded the countys best fifth wicket stand with a partnership of 277 in the match against New Zealand at Canterbury. Ames was involved in another important batting partnership against the New Zealanders later that summer when he and Gubby Allen put on 246 for the eighth wicket in the Test match at Lords.

In 1949, Kent and England wicket-keeper Godfrey Evans claimed nine victims (eight caught and one stumped) in the match against the tourists at Canterbury.

NICKNAMES

Many players in the clubs history have been fondly known by their nickname. They include:

Edward Humphreys	1899-1920	Punter
Frank Woolley	1906-1938	Stork
Alfred Freeman	1914-1936	Tich
Charles Marriott	1924-1937	Father
Howard Levett	1930-1947	Hopper
Brian Luckhurst	1958-1976	Lucky
Derek Underwood	1963-1987	Deadly

NORTHAMPTONSHIRE

Northamptonshire, founded in 1820, have never won the County Championship but have been second four times. They have won the Gillette Cup in 1976 and in 1992, under the title of the Nat West Trophy, and the Benson and Hedges Cup in 1980.

In May 1907, Colin Blythe accomplished the remarkable performance of taking ten wickets in an innings and 17 in the match — all in one day at Northampton. At one time, Northants were four runs for seven wickets, Blythe having taken seven wickets for one run. They managed to make 60 in their first innings but were bowled out for 39 in the second. Blythe took ten for 30 and seven for 18, all in less than a day s play during 31.1 overs.

During the countys Championship-winning season of 1913, there was the unusual sight at Northampton of two Kent players in direct opposition to their brothers. At one stage C N Woolley and John Seymour were batting against their respective brothers, Frank and James.

In the game against Northamptonshire at the Crabble in 1935, Father Marriott bowled a remarkable 624 balls. He bowled 55 maidens, ten of them in succession, and failed by only six balls to equal the record number ever bowled in a county match.

NOTTINGHAMSHIRE

Founded in 1841, Nottinghamshire were undoubtedly the strongest team in the country in the late nineteenth century, taking ten unofficial county titles between 1865 and 1886. Since those days they have had occasional successes, taking the Championship again in 1907, 1929, 1981 and 1987. They won their first one-day title in 1987 when they captured the Nat West Trophy and followed this up with the Benson and Hedges Cup in 1989 and the Sunday League in 1991.

Towards the end of the 1889 season, Kent entertained Nottinghamshire at Beckenham. The visitors were favourites to win and carry off the County Championship but in their second innings they were dismissed for 35 on a wicket of uneven bounce, leaving Kent to make just 52 for victory. They were struggling at 35 for six when George Hearne entered the fray, batting for almost two hours to score 14 not out and leading Kent to a four-wicket victory. This result meant that the Championship was tied by Lancashire, Nottinghamshire and Surrey.

In the match at Dover in 1922, George Collins had taken all of Nottinghamshire s nine wickets to fall when he had the chance to catch the tenth off a ball from Tich Freeman. Slow to react, he put the chance down. Suspecting that the crowd would think he had dropped it on purpose, he was mortified. However, in the following over Tich Freeman took a brilliant catch to provide Collins with all ten wickets for 65 runs.

Another outstanding bowling performance in a match against Nottinghamshire came in 1959 when Alan Brown, playing against the county of his birth, took four wickets in five balls.

ONE-DAY FINISHES

Kents game against England at Lords on 5 July 1858 was completed on the first day. Kent were dismissed for 33 and though they managed to bowl England out for 73, they could only muster 41 in their second innings, leaving Englands openers just two to make for victory.

The match against Sussex in June 1919 was scheduled for the old Angel ground at Tonbridge. Rain washed out play on the Friday but Woolley and Fairservice soon made up for lost time the following day, having Sussex five for five. The lower order managed to add 55 but the innings was completed in 26 overs with Woolley returning six for 33 and Fairservice four for 21. For Kent, Hubble made 71 and Woolley 59 as Kent declared at 261 for six. Sussex were all out in their second innings for 78, Woolley taking six for 28 and having match figures of 12 for 61. Kent won by an innings and 123 runs.

In June 1960, Kent beat Worcestershire inside a day by an innings and 101 runs. Kent batted first and were all out for 187. After just eight overs, Worcestershire were nine for six but rallied slightly to be all out for 25 — Halfyard took four for seven and Brown six for 12. Enforcing the follow-on, Kent dismissed half the Worcestershire side for just 18 runs but again the lower order hit out freely to take the score to 61 — Halfyard having five for 20 and Brown three for 22, giving him a match analysis of nine for 34.

OVERSEAS PLAYERS

One of the most popular overseas players to represent Kent was John Shepherd (1966-1981). The West Indian all-rounder, who appeared in five Tests, went on to score 9,401 runs and take 832 wickets for Kent before moving on to Gloucestershire.

Pakistan all-rounder Asif Iqbal (1968-1982), played alongside John Shepherd in many games for Kent. He was a batsman of quality and a bowler who could cut or swing the ball. He scored 13,231 runs and captured

73 wickets for the hop county and will always be remembered by Kent followers as a constant and thrilling match winner.

Bernard Julien (1970-1977) was spotted by Colin Cowdrey when he visited Trinidad with the Duke of Norfolks team. Cowdrey promptly signed the youngster for Kent. Sadly his early games for the county were overshadowed by personal problems. His father had died just before he left Trinidad and he worried about his mother coping on her own. He went on to score 2,057 runs and take 198 wickets for Kent as well as appearing in 24 Tests for the West Indies.

Another West Indian, Eldine Baptiste (1981-1987) made his first-class debut for Kent against Oxford University before, a year later, playing for the Leeward Islands. His best season for Kent was 1983 when he hit a career best 136 not out against Yorkshire. Capped nine times by the West Indies, he scored 2,974 runs and took 207 wickets for Kent.

Terry Alderman who took a record 42 wickets for Australia in his first Test series against England, elected to join a rebel tour of South Africa earning himself a three-year ban. Stints with Kent (1984-1986) and Gloucestershire made him a master of English conditions. Alderman, who appeared in 41 tests for Australia, took 174 wickets at 20.72 runs apiece in two seasons with Kent.

South African Roy Pienaar (1987-1989), who had played for Transvaal at the age of sixteen, spent three seasons with Kent, topping the batting averages with 1,239 runs at 59.00 in his final season with the county.

West Indians Hartley Alleyne and Anthony Merrick also played for Kent but neither set the world alight. Yet both bowlers had performed hat-tricks for their previous counties, Worcestershire and Warwickshire.

South African Test bowler Fanie De Villiers spent the summer of 1990 playing for Kent. He was hampered by injury and just took 25 wickets at 39.68 runs each.

West Indian all-rounder, Carl Hooper, first played for Kent in 1992 and has, in five seasons cricket, scored a total of 6,714 runs and taken 154 wickets. His highest score of 236 not out came against Glamorgan at Canterbury in 1993. At the time of writing, Hooper has appeared in 80 Test for the West Indies, scoring 4,153 runs and capturing 93 wickets.

Sri Lankan Aravinda de Silva played for Kent in 1995. He had a magnificent season, topping the batting averages with 1,661 runs at 59.32 including a highest score of 256 against Derbyshire at Maidstone. In the Benson and Hedges Cup Final against Lancashire he scored 112 out of Kents total of 239 and, although on the losing side, was named Man-of-the-Match. Not surprisingly he was also named as one of *Wisden's* Five Cricketers of the Year.

Paul Strang of Zimbabwe spent just one season as Kents overseas player but his performances in 1997 of 588 runs and 61 wickets were very disappointing.

Indian Test star, Rahul David, played for Kent in the summer of 2000 and was the only batsman to pass the 1,000 run mark, topping the batting averages with 1,039 runs at 49.47. Kents overseas player for 2001 was South African batsman Daryll Cullinan.

OXFORD UNIVERSITY

When Kent met Oxford University at the Parks in 1982, they equalled the feat of four centuries in an innings, first achieved against Somerset in 1908. It was accomplished against Oxford University by the first four batsmen in the batting order — Bob Woolmer (126) Neil Taylor (127) Chris Tavare (125) and Mark Benson (120).

P

PAKISTAN

Kent first met Pakistan at Canterbury in 1954 when the tourists won by nine wickets with Zulfiqar Ahmed having match figures of 12 for 114.

The next three games were drawn with the last of them, in 1971, being the last first-class match staged at the Bat and Ball Ground, Gravesend.

Despite a century by Colin Cowdrey, Kent lost again by nine wickets in the 1974 meeting. Kents only success in this fixture came in 1987 when they won by an innings and 57 runs. No Kent batsman reached three figures but they declared their first innings at 403 for eight with Tavare 87, Chris Cowdrey 75, Hinks 70 and Penn 53, the leading scorers. Alan Igglesden with five for 60 made sure the home side won.

PARTNERSHIPS

Once, when Kent wanted 218 to win against the clock, the opening batsmen were Frank Woolley and Bill Ashdown. The score mounted rapidly with Woolley striking the ball superbly. At the end of an over, Ashdown went down the pitch to have a word with his partner. Don t hit so many sixes. It wastes too much time, he said.

PHEBEY, ARTHUR

After making a promising start for Kent when the game resumed after the Second World War, Arthur Phebey decided to leave the staff for a time and in doing so lost much valuable experience. He later returned to the fold, but it was 1951 before he established himself fully in the side. During that season, he carried his bat for 89 out of Kents 209 against Worcestershire at Kidderminster, the first of four occasions he did so.

Phebey was an elegant opening batsman, helping bring solidarity to the Kent batting line-up. He achieved over 1,000 runs in a season for nine consecutive years, with a best of 1,737 runs at an average of 33.40 in 1959. Yet despite his consistency at county level, he was never considered to represent his country. In 1960, Phebey shared in the second highest partnership for Kent s third wicket with the adventurous Bob Wilson. They put on 304 runs against Glamorgan at Blackheath.

Phebey retired at the end of the 1961 season, after scoring 14,299 runs at an average of 25.90 and a top score of 157. He then became heavily involved with Kent cricket, being a member of the General and Executive Committee. A belated honour came his way when he was made a life vice-president of the county.

RECORD WICKET PARTNERSHIPS

The county s highest partnerships for each wicket is as follows:

1st	300	N Taylor and M Benson	v Derbyshire at Canterbury 1991
2nd	366	S Hinks and N Taylor	v Middlesex at Canterbury 1990
3rd	321*	A Hearne and J Mason	v Nottinghamshire at Trent Bridge 1899
4th	368	A de Silva and G Cowdrey	v Derbyshire at Maidstone 1995
5th	277	F Woolley and L Ames	v New Zealand at Canterbury 1931
6th	315	P A de Silva and M Ealham	v Nottinghamshire at Trent Bridge 1995
7th	248	A Day and E.Humphreys	v Somerset at Taunton 1908
8th	157	A Hilder and A Wright	v Essex at Gravesend 1924
9th	171	M Ealham and P Strang	v Nottinghamshire at Trent Bridge 1997
10th	235	F Woolley and A Fielder	v Warwickshire at Stourbridge 1909

RICHARDSON, PETER

Like his brother Dick, Peter Richardson joined Worcestershire as an amateur straight from Hereford Cathedral School, having gained a place in the Minor Counties side in 1949. It was the summer of 1952 which marked the turning point in Richardson s career when an opening partner was needed for Don Kenyon. He was given six matches to prove his worth and following a series of high scores, he never looked back.

In 1956, Richardson scored hundreds in three consecutive innings and was selected for the first of thirty-four Tests against Australia at Trent Bridge. Scoring 81 and 73 on his debut, he kept his place for the whole of the series, scoring the first of five Test hundreds at Old Trafford, a match England won by an innings and 170 runs.

Richardson was an automatic choice in the England side for the next three years but after a disastrous tour of Australia in 1958-59, he lost his place. That loss of form coincided with the end of his career at Worcester where he had just completed a three-year spell as captain.

On joining Kent, Richardson, who employed a minimal backlift and was an accomplished manipulator of the nudge, push and steer, spent a year qualifying for the county. On his Kent debut against Cambridge University, before he had qualified, he was out without scoring. However, he quickly adapted to his new surroundings and developed a much more fluent style. Sometimes he would revert back to resolute defence and stolen singles, yet there were instances when he broke free of his shackles and scored a hundred before lunch — which he did on four occasions.

Richardsons best season for Kent was 1961 when he scored 2,119 runs at 38.52 and hit five centuries. He played his last game in 1965, having scored 9,975 runs at 35.88 for the hop county.

RIDGWAY, FRED

Fred Ridgway was a great trier and, although never truly fast, he could certainly be hostile. He often had to bowl long spells without a rest and taking this into consideration it is not surprising that his bowling figures were sometimes quite expensive.

In 1949 he had his most successful season in terms of taking wickets, 105 at 23.32 runs apiece. This was a season when he also showed his worth with the bat, helping Brian Edrich put on 161 for the ninth wicket in the game against Sussex at Tunbridge Wells — Ridgway ending with 89 runs to his name.

In 1951, in the match against Derbyshire, Ridgway became the first Kent bowler since 1862 to take four wickets in four balls.

He was in his prime when many other quick bowlers were available to play for England. However, he was chosen for the MCC tour of India in 1951-52 and he seemed an ideal choice, being able to bowl for a long time. He played in five Tests on that tour but only took seven wickets at the high cost of 54.14 runs each.

There are a number of examples of Ridgway disappointing with his opening spell but coming out on top when he came back for a second bite. In the 1952 match against Essex at Clacton, Dickie Dodds had taken

Ridgway apart — his figures being 0 for 60. His second spell was a totally different story, his fine accurate bowling bringing him a final analysis of eight for 112.

In his later years, when he had lost some of his pace, he increased his control and therefore became a much better bowler. In 1958 he took seven for 42 against Oxford University including the second hat-trick of his career. His best figures were eight for 39 against Gloucestershire.

Fred Ridgway possesses an unwanted distinction — as he ran in to deliver his first ball in a match played in the presence of the Queen, he fell flat on his face . . .

S

SEMI-FINALS

Up to the end of the 2001 season, Kent had appeared in twenty semi-finals of limited-overs competitions. These included seven Gillette/Nat West Trophy matches and thirteen Benson and Hedges Cup games.

SEYMOUR, JAMES

Although he was born in Sussex, Jim Seymours long residency in Pembury made him eligible to play for Kent. He made his debut for the county in 1902 but it was some two years later before he made his mark, scoring 1,166 runs including two centuries.

Seymour passed 1,000 runs in a season on sixteen occasions and in 1907 he scored 204 against Hampshire at Tonbridge — then his highest individual score for the county. In 1911 he repeated his double-century of four years earlier, hitting an unbeaten 218 against Essex at Leyton. In terms of runs scored Seymours best season was 1913 when he finished with a total of 2,088 at an average of just under 40. He never took part in a Test though that summer saw him make the first of three appearances for the Gentlemen against the Players, making 80 in the second innings at the Oval.

Seymour never rose to the highest level of representative cricket because in his day the standard was very high indeed, yet he was a player of the highest class in terms of county cricket. He played with an upright yet slightly open stance, possessing probably the widest range of strokes of any batsman in the country. His flash past cover-point was a pure delight and he excelled also at the old-fashioned full-blooded leg-side hit.

As a slip fielder, he was on a par with the greatest to occupy this position; the combination of Huish, Seymour, Mason, Blaker and Hutchings behind the wicket being one of the most difficult to pass.

Seymour continued to be one of Kents leading players in the years after the First World War and in 1923, he scored 143 and 105 not out in the match against Essex at Leyton. After retiring from the first-class scene in 1926, having scored 26,818 runs at an average of 32.62, Seymour became a hero to every professional cricketer. He had received a demand for income tax on that part of his benefit money which accrued from entry fees paid at the gate. On appeal, the Income Tax Commissioner decided in his favour. The Crown took the case to the High Court where the Commissioners decision was upheld. The Crown then went to the Court of Appeal and won. Seymour appealed to the Lords and won his case.

Shortly before his death, he had accepted an engagement as coach at Epsom College.

SHEPHERD, JOHN

In 1964, Colin Cowdrey and Les Ames were touring the West Indies when they came across a good young cricketer with a super personality — his name was John Shepherd. They invited him to come to England and play 2nd XI cricket for Kent. Within two years he had established himself as an important member of the Kent 1st XI.

Shepherd was awarded his county cap in 1977 and he was instrumental in Kent winning that seasons Gillette Cup. In the close season he returned to play for Barbados in the Shell Shield, obviously hoping to force his way into the West Indies side. However, his hopes were dashed when he missed an attempted hook shot off David Brown with the ball shattering his cheekbone.

In 1968, when Kent were runners-up in the County Championship, Shepherd made a great impression in his first full season with 1,157 runs and 96 wickets. The following summer he was an automatic choice for the West Indies side to tour England. Playing in all of the Tests, he topped the bowling averages of this three-match series with 12 wickets at 22.16 runs each.

In 1970 Kent celebrated their centenary year by winning the County Championship. Shepherd took 84 wickets — more than any of the other Kent bowlers. He only appeared in two more Test matches for the West Indies but he continued to both score runs and take wickets for Kent and in 1973, despite the reduction in first-class matches, he was not far short of the double .

He also became the first black cricketer to tour South Africa with the

John Shepherd scored runs as well as took wickets for Kent.

Derrick Robins team. In 1975-76 he played for Rhodesia in the Currie Cup and also had a successful season playing Grade cricket for Footscray, the Melbourne club, picking up more runs and wickets than anyone else.

John Shepherd is probably the best of his type of bowler that Kent have had on their staff since the war. He took 832 wickets and he could swing the ball both ways, move it off the seam, and possessed an extremely good fast delivery.

At the end of the 1981 season, he moved to Gloucestershire where after a few seasons, he became their coach.

SMALLEST PLAYER

The distinction of being Kents smallest player goes to Tich Freeman. Standing just 5ft 2ins, the Lewisham-born bowler wrote numerous new entries in the record book, finishing with 3,340 wickets at 17.64 runs each in his 506 games for Kent.

SOMERSET

Founded in 1875, Somerset went 100 years without winning a trophy before they won five one-day titles — the Benson and Hedges Cup in 1981 and 1982, the 1979 Gillette Cup and Sunday League and the Nat West Trophy in 1983. Last summer they won the inaugural C and G Trophy.

During the summer of 1891, one of the wettest on record, William Best turned in a unique bowling performance. In what was his only appearance for the county, the slow right-arm bowler performed the hat-trick.

In 1908, in the match at Taunton, Edward Humphreys and Arthur Day scored 248 for the seventh wicket , still a club record and the last 201 runs of this partnership were scored in just an hour and a quarter. This was also the only occasion in a County Championship match when Kent had four batsmen scoring a century — Seymour making 129, Woolley 105, Day 118, and Humphreys 149. Kent won by an innings and 114 runs.

SOUTH AFRICA

Kents first match with the South Africans was played at Beckenham in 1901 and was marked by a century opening stand in each innings for the county by Cuthbert Burnup and Edward Humphreys. In the tourists second innings, both Colin Blythe and Bill Bradley took three wickets in four balls and Kent won by seven wickets.

In the match at Canterbury in 1904, James Seymour, fielding at slip, took six catches in an innings, a feat which has been equalled by only one Kent player since — Stuart Leary, himself a South African — against Cambridge University in 1958.

When the South Africans visited Canterbury in 1965, after winning the Test series at the Oval, Graeme Pollock scored a brilliant double-century, thrashing the Kent attack to all parts of the ground.

SRI LANKA

During the match against the Sri Lankans at Canterbury in 1979, Kents opening batsman Neil Taylor scored a chanceless century on what was his first-class debut for the county.

SUNDAY LEAGUE

The Sunday League was introduced in 1969 and Kent became particularly adept at the 40-over game, winning the Championship three times in the first seven years.

Their first title came in 1972 when they beat Worcestershire on the final day of the season. Worcestershire s total of 190 represented the highest made in the John Player League games against Kent all season. Perhaps the most surprising feature of the innings was the ease with which Underwood was hit. Although he dismissed Stewart, to become the second bowler after Keith Boyce to take 100 wickets, his eight overs cost 61 runs. In reply Johnson struck some early boundaries before a second wicket partnership of 108 from 22 overs by Luckhurst and Nicholls virtually settled the contest which Kent won by five wickets. This win, their sixth in succession, took them past Leicestershire, who had led the table for twelve weeks.

Kent proved that winning the title in 1972 was no fluke by winning it again the following year. They got their nose in front early and apart from a defeat at Bournemouth where Trevor Jesty was in outstanding form, Kent just kept on winning. Mike Denness was certainly lucky with the toss for nine out of twelve victories came after Kent had won the toss and batted first.

On the Sunday after winning the Benson and Hedges Final, Kent annihilated Northamptonshire. Kent scored so quickly that after 30 overs, a number of Northamptonshire members suggested they declare. Kent reached 257 for seven and then bowled Northamptonshire out for 67. After a 29 run win over Leicestershire in a televised game, Kent ended the season four points ahead of runners-up Yorkshire who had a glorious late run in.

There can surely have never been as dramatic an ending to Kent s third John Player League Championship in 1976. The destination of the trophy was in doubt almost until the last ball had been bowled.

The BBC decided that Kent had won and its helicopter set off for Maidstone for the presentation ceremony. But down in Cardiff Graham Burgess was making an heroic effort to bring the trophy to Somerset and prove the BBC wrong in eliminating his county from the final outcome.

He just failed and so Kents success was by the narrowest of margins — a run rate of 4.988 against 4.560 by Essex, each side having won five away matches. In addition, Leicestershire, Somerset and Sussex had, like Kent and Essex, finished on 40 points.

Kents fourth Sunday League title was won in 1995, again by virtue of a run-rate superior to that of Warwickshire and Worcestershire, both of whom finished like Kent with 50 points.

In 2001, Kent picked up the Norwich Union League title from Leicestershires pocket as the Foxes went down by five wickets to Nottinghamshire at Trent Bridge. The Kent Spitfires rounded off their late surge with a nine run victory over Warwickshire at Edgbaston. After making 211 for six, Kent were left to defend 218 in 40 overs after rain brought the Duckworth-Lewis formula into play. Kents Andrew Symonds took five for 18 as Warwickshire never came close to making the 18 runs to win off the last over. As Matthew Fleming said after receiving the trophy: It was a triumph of character and determination. We just had to hang on in there .

Kents Sunday League records include:

Highest Innings Total	327 for 6 v Leicestershire at Canterbury 1993
Lowest Innings Total	83 v Middlesex at Lords 1984
Highest Individual Innings	45 by Carl Hooper v Leicestershire at Leicester in 1996
Best Bowling Performance	6 for 9 by Bob Woolmer v Derbyshire at Chesterfield in 1979
Highest Partnership	241 by Trevor Ward and Aravinda de Silva v Surrey at Canterbury in 1995
Most Runs in a Season	854 at 65.69 by Carl Hooper 1993
Most Wickets in a Season	32 at 16.87 by Bob Woolmer 1970

SURREY

Founded in 1845, Surrey won three unofficial titles before capturing the first official County Championship in 1890. The county have won seventeen Championships, including an unprecedented run of seven successive wins from 1952 to 1958. Their last Championship success came in 2000. The county have also won all the one-day competitions, winning the Benson and Hedges Cup in 1974, the Nat West Trophy in 1982 and the Sunday League in 1996.

Charles Thornton, who had established a reputation as a tremendous hitter produced a remarkable shot in the match against Surrey at Canterbury in 1871. Two runs were completed and a third begun before the ball fell to the ground after one of his powerful blows.

His old friend Lord Harris in 1885, batted for more than 35 minutes in the match against Surrey at the Oval using only his left-hand because his right-hand in which he had broken a small bone earlier in the innings was in a sling.

Another player to sustain an injury in the Kent v Surrey matches was Walter Wright. At the Oval in 1890 in trying to make a return catch, he sustained a compound fracture of the left thumb. He was taken to St Thomass Hospital in great agony and was detained for five weeks, during which his thumb was saved by careful treatment after amputation had been feared.

Cuthbert Burnup had the unusual distinction in 1900 of making his 49 in the match against Surrey at Canterbury over part of each of the three days because of interruptions by the weather. The following summer in the match at the Oval, the first over bowled by Ted Dillon saw a single scored off each delivery, with the fielder in every instance being Cuthbert Burnup.

The match at the Oval in 1905 was tied after Harry Murrell at cover point rubbed his hands on his trousers before catching a skier from Surreys Smith.

When Colin Blythe performed the first of his two hat-tricks against Surrey at Blackheath in 1910, he had five wickets for no runs in ten balls including four in five balls.

In 1911, wicketkeeper Fred Huish claimed ten dismissals in the match against Surrey at the Oval — one caught and nine stumped. This was then a record for stumpings in a first-class match. That season was a good one for Frank Woolley. He made 42 out of 78 in 28 minutes, hitting six fours and a two off eight balls from Hitch and breaking his bat in going for another big hit off the next delivery. Then in the return against Surrey, he took seven for 9 — the wickets being taken in 24 balls for a cost of just five runs.

SUSSEX

Founded in 1839, Sussex have seven times been County Championship runners-up but have never managed to win the title. They won the first two Gillette Cups and then won the trophy again in 1978. They won the Sunday League in 1982 and the Nat West Trophy in 1986.

The match against Sussex at Tonbridge in 1919 — the first season of county cricket following the First World War — play finished on the second day after rain had washed out the whole of the first day. Kent scored 261 for six declared and then dismissed Sussex for 60 and 78 to win by an innings and 123 runs.

Tich Freeman produced a couple of outstanding bowling performances against Sussex. He took nine for 87 at Hastings in 1920, the home captain declaring before he could take the tenth. In 1922 he took 17 wickets in the game at Hove, including nine for 11 in the first innings as Sussex were bowled out for 47. In the return fixture he claimed another 12 victims to finish with 29 wickets for 138 runs in the two matches against Sussex for an unbelievable average of 4.74.

Sussex were Kents opponents in their first limited overs match at Tunbridge Wells on 22 May 1963. Sussex amassed 314 for seven in their 65 overs with Ken Suttle scoring 104. Despite making a dreadful start, Kents Peter Richardson made 127, a performance which earned him the Man-of-the-Match award although it was Sussex who won the game and went on to win the Gillette Cup.

In 1984 Kent and Sussex were involved in a tied match. It was the only occasion that Derek Underwood made a century after coming in as nightwatchman. The wicket at Hastings was Deadly s favourite and in the Sunday League game he took six for 12 to become the second bowler to reach 300 wickets in that competition.

TALLEST PLAYER

Almost certain to lay claim to the distinction of being Kents tallest player is Norman Graham. Standing 6ft 7ins, the Hexham-born pace bowler took 600 wickets at a cost of 22.43 runs apiece and a best of eight for 20 against Essex at Brentwood in 1969.

Chris Tavare.

TAVARE, CHRIS

It was obvious during Chris Tavares time at Oxford University that he was destined for a great career in both county and international cricket. He won Blues at Oxford from 1975 to 1977, although in 1973 he hit a hundred for the English Schools against All India Schools at Edgbaston and made his Kent debut in 1974. Having hit the first of his twenty-nine centuries for Kent against Nottinghamshire at Canterbury in 1977, Tavare scored 1,432 runs at 44.75 the following summer — his first full season in the Kent side. He was a remarkably consistent batsman who could both anchor an innings or give Kent a push with his stylish stroke play. It was evident in those early years that Kent were soon going to be losing him to England for Test matches.

In 1980, Tavare had a chance at a

higher level when he was chosen to represent England in the one-day international against the West Indies. The match was at Headingley, Tavare scoring 82 not out. This fine innings won him selection for the first two Tests.

In 1981 Tavare had his best season to date, scoring 1,591 runs at 54.86 and winning a recall to the England side for the Old Trafford Test where he scored 69 and 78. In this match he batted for something like twelve hours, his second 50 being the slowest in a Test in England at the time. Also in 1981, Tavare showed the other side of his batting technique. In the Lambert and Butler Floodlit Cup at Crystal Palaces Football Ground, he hit a century off just twenty-seven balls.

In 1981-82 Tavare toured India where he scored his first Test hundred, 149 at Delhi. Although he batted at No.3 for Kent the England selectors asked him to open. This he did, and at Lords in 1982, in the Test against Pakistan, he broke his slow speed record, taking some 350 minutes to reach his fifty. His innings of 82 in just over 400 minutes almost saved England from defeat and showed his skill, courage and concentration at the highest level.

He was appointed captain of Kent in 1983, and he led the county to two losing Lords finals. On ceasing to be captain, he signed a new four year contract and in each of those seasons, he passed the 1,000 run mark. In 1988, his last season with the county, he helped Kent to within one point of the County Championship. He had scored 14,201 runs at an average of 37.97 when he left to end his first-class career with Somerset.

TAYLOR, NEIL

Neil Taylor made his Kent debut against the touring Sri Lankans in 1979 when, by scoring 110, he became the first Kent batsman for thirty-two years to achieve the feat of scoring a debut century.

During the formative part of his career Taylor was stuck with the label of being a slow scorer, but gradually he cast off that image to develop into one of the countrys most consistent scorers. In 1982 his devastating form brought him five centuries, in all competitions, before the middle of June. That summer he appeared in the role of twelfth man for England and took a spectacular catch to dismiss Indias Sundeep Patil at the Oval. His form that season led to him playing for the England B side against

Pakistan but though he continued to score freely for Kent, he could not make the grade to Test cricket.

Taylor, who scored three successive centuries in the Benson and Hedges Cup competition, went on to score 17,721 runs for Kent at an average of 39.82, making his highest score of 204 against Surrey at Canterbury in 1990, a match in which he scored 142 in the games second innings.

TEST CRICKETERS

Kents most capped England player is Colin Cowdrey who won 114 caps. The full list of Kent players who represented England at Test level is:

Charlie Absalom	1	Frank Hearne	2
Les Ames	47	George Hearne	1
Mark Benson	1	Kenneth Hutchings	7
Ivo Bligh	4	Alan Igglesden	3
Colin Blythe	19	Alan Knott	95
Bill Bradley	2	Geoffrey Legge	5
Alan Brown	2	Howard Levett	1
Douglas Carr	1	Brian Luckhurst	21
Percy Chapman	26	Martin McCague	3
Stanley Christopherson	1	Francis Mackinnon	1
Chris Cowdrey	6	Charles Marriott	1
Colin Cowdrey	114	Fred Martin	2
Mike Denness	28	Jack Martin	1
Graham Dilley	26	Jack Mason	5
Mark Ealham	8	Min Patel	2
Richard Ellison	11	Frank Penn	1
Godfrey Evans	91	Peter Richardson	9
John Evans	1	Fred Ridgway	5
Arthur Fagg	5	Chris Tavare	30
Arthur Fielder	6	Edward Tylecote	6
Tich Freeman	12	Derek Underwood	86
Wally Hardinge	1	Bryan Valentine	7
Lord Harris	4	George Wood	3
Dean Headley	15	Frank Woolley	64
Alec Hearne	1	Bob Woolmer	19

THORNTON, CHARLES

It was at Eton that Charles Thornton began to show his sporting prowess. He won the school Fives, the Double Racquets, the Weight and Throwing the Cricket Ball. After going up to Trinity College, Cambridge, he played in the XI for four years 1869-1872, the last year as captain. In the year he went up to Cambridge Thornton was a fast under-arm bowler and once, when playing for his own XI against Kings School, Canterbury, his sneaks took all ten wickets.

Thornton was a real character and is probably the biggest hitter English cricket has ever had. He delighted in big hits, whether it be the first ball or last ball of a match. In those days it was quite common to measure drives and not uncommon for Thornton to hit some 140 or 150 yards. In fact, one of his hits at Canterbury was such a colossal drive that it measured 152 yards. Thorntons largest measured hit, made at Hove, was just short of 169 yards. He once hit nine sixes over the canvas that enclosed the ground at Tunbridge Wells, and at Canterbury he hit each ball of one four ball over from Vyell Walker out of the ground.

Without doubt, Scarborough was Thorntons favourite ground. In 1894 he was presented with a silver loving cup subscribed for by the members of Scarborough Cricket Club. In 1921 he was made a Freeman of the Borough of Scarborough where he organised several games and was, in the main, responsible for the introduction of the cricket festival there.

Like many players of his day, Thornton regarded cricket purely as a game rather than the serious business it has become today. In six seasons with Kent, he appeared in only eighteen matches, hitting three hundreds. He never wore pads and only wore gloves (and then only once) towards the end of his career.

Thornton was also an avid film-goer and used to carry an enormous black wallet containing newspaper reports on every murder case for the past twenty-five years.

He had to be watched when the coin was tossed. Thornton used to call woman which could be either heads (Queen Victoria) or tails (Britannia), and before the other captain had realised what was happening Thornton would have decided to bat.

He was also a keen motorist and after he had finished playing cricket, he travelled through Japan, Siberia and Russia. When the war broke out he was in Berlin and just avoided being captured. With his death in 1929 at the age of seventy-nine, there passed a great personality in the history of cricket.

TIED MATCHES

Kent have been involved in four tied County Championship matches. Their first experience of such an occurrence came in 1847 when Surrey (112 and 160) tied with Kent (127 and 145) at the Oval. Surrey were Kents opponents in 1905 when the hop county, chasing 85 for victory, were bowled out for 84. In those games, a match was considered to be tied if the scores were level after the fourth innings, even if the side batting last had wickets in hand when stumps were drawn on the final day. In 1948, Law 22 was amended and ruled that a game is regarded as a tie when the scores are equal at the conclusion of play but only if the match has been played out.

In 1950, in the match against Hampshire at Southampton, Kent were dismissed for 162 with only Godfrey Evans, who hit a swashbuckling innings of 71, having any answer to the spin of Knott and Dare. The home side gained a narrow advantage of 18 runs on first innings. Kent lost both openers before the slender arrears had been wiped off, and totalled 170 to leave Hampshire needing 153 for victory. With Doug Wright virtually unplayable, Hampshires last pair still needed 22 to win but despite edging closer and closer to victory, Arthur Fagg at slip held on to the chance that gave Kent a tie — the first in the County Championship since the alteration to the system of scoring two years previously.

During the summer of 1984, Kent were involved in two tied matches. Against Sussex at Hastings, the home side scored 143 and 192 and Kent replied with 92 and 243. In the match against Northamptonshire, Kent declared their second innings closed at 204 for five, setting the home side 331 for victory but despite a valiant effort, they were all out for 330, leaving the scores tied.

Kents last tied match in 1991 was against Sussex at Hove. They scored 381 and 408 for seven declared, leaving Sussex, who made 353 in their first innings, 437 to win. In a high scoring contest they were all out for 436.

TODD, LESLIE

When Leslie Todd entered county cricket with Kent in 1927, he was hailed as another Frank Woolley. Yet he was probably the games greatest enigma. When runs were needed quickly, Todd would keep one end completely shut up. If it was vital that Kent did not lose another wicket, he would set about the bowling, unleashing an array of unorthodox strokes and more than likely get out. His captain and team-mates would obviously be furious but nobody could be angry with him for long.

He often failed to make the most of his talents because he had an extraordinary temper. From 1933 to the outbreak of the Second World War he succeeded in reaching 1,000 runs a season with the exception of 1938. His best season was 1934 when he scored 1,897 runs in the Championship at an average of 52.69.

In 1936, Todd achieved the cricketers double, scoring 1,211 runs and taking 102 wickets. He was a complete all-rounder. As a bowler he was initially a slow bowler but in the seasons prior to the war he bowled left-arm medium-quick with a devilish late in-swinger. He went on to take 555 wickets at a cost of 27.38 runs apiece.

When cricket resumed after the hostilities, Todd did little bowling because he had back trouble. Despite his temperament and the loss of six years to the Second World War, when he was at his peak, he still went on to score 19,407 runs at 31.50. His best season was 1947 when he amassed 2,057 runs at 44.71 and shared in a second wicket partnership of 273 with Les Ames in the match against Essex at Maidstone.

Few players have had such talent for the game of cricket, yet Leslie Todd never played for England. Kent could and did accommodate this wayward genius but the Test selectors were a little wary of choosing someone whose approach to cricket was, to say the least, unpredictable.

TOURS

At the end of the 1903 season, Kent made history by being the first side to be invited to play in America. With players such as Bill Bradley, Colin Blythe, Arthur Fielder, Jack Mason, Cuthbert Burnup and Ted Dillon in their ranks, they won all four matches they played in Philadelphia.

TROUGHTON, LIONEL

When Ted Dillon resigned the Kent captaincy after the successful season of 1913, the county approached Lionel Troughton as his replacement. He was at the time captain of the Kent 2nd XI and had not been awarded his county cap.

During his first season in charge, Troughton, who was a much-respected leader, hit the only century of his Kent career, 104 against Oxford University. He held the position of captain until 1923 when he handed over to Captain (later Lord) Cornwallis. That same year, Troughton took over the post of business manager at Kent when the beloved Tom Pawley died at Canterbury at the beginning of August.

Lionel Troughton was never a prolific scoring batsman, though he often made useful scores coming in lower down the order. He did score another hundred in his first-class career — when he was a member of the MCC party to Argentina in 1911-12, captained by Lancashire's Archie MacLaren. In the match against the Combined Camps at Buenos Aires, Troughton scored 112 not out.

He was a big influence on Tich Freeman in his early days at Kent. He would set his field for him, discussing and explaining what he was doing. He taught Freeman a great deal, all the while using tact and firmness.

A notable figure in Kent cricketing circles, Lionel Troughton died in 1933, still in the post of general manager of the county club.

TUNBRIDGE WELLS

The Nevill Cricket ground is the home of Tunbridge Wells CC, which was founded in 1782, and Blue Mantles CC, founded in 1895. Tunbridge Wells CC previously played at the Higher Common ground in Fir Tree Road between 1786 and 1884 until it moved to Nevill Gate in 1895.

The Nevill Gate ground was acquired on a lease of 99 years from the Eridge Park Estate of the Marquess of Abergavenny. It was first opened in 1898 by the Marquess and the first Kent match was in 1901 when Lancashire were the visitors.

During the First World War, the Nevill ground became a picketing area for the cavalry with several hundred horses tethered on the playing area. Lord Harris, before he became Governor of Bombay, frequently led the county side on this ground during his later years. Here it was that Colin Blythe bowled 12 overs against Sussex and gave away only one run in an hour. Here too, Charlie Barnett of Gloucestershire chopped a fastish ball onto his stumps, where, by some quirk of fate, the bails remained firmly lodged.

In 1983 an international match was staged on the ground when the Prudential Cup match between India and Zimbabwe followed the usual Kent and Sussex Championship match. Kapil Dev hit 175 not out in that competition, the highest individual innings in the history of the World Cup until beaten by Viv Richards in Karachi in 1987.

TWO HUNDRED WICKETS

Only Tich Freeman has achieved this feat for Kent and he did so on seven occasions.

Year	Wickets	Average
1928	246	17.58
1929	214	17.42
1930	260	15.97
1931	257	15.29
1932	226	15.23
1933	262	14.74
1935	212	21.51

TWO THOUSAND RUNS

The first batsman to notch up 2,000 runs in a season for Kent was Wally Hardinge in 1913 when he scored 2,018 runs at 42.93. The highest number of runs scored in any one season for the county is 2,894 by Frank Woolley in 1928. The full list of Kent players scoring 2,000 runs in county matches in a season is:

Batsman	Runs	Average	Year
Frank Woolley	2,894	59.06	1928
Frank Woolley	2,540	50.80	1934
Wally Hardinge	2,446	59.65	1928
Les Ames	2,428	55.18	1933
Arthur Fagg	2,420	55.00	1948
Frank Woolley	2,339	41.76	1935
Arthur Fagg	2,322	52.77	1938

Batsman	Runs	Average	Year
Bill Ashdown	2,247	43.21	1928
Wally Hardinge	2,234	47.53	1926
Les Ames	2,156	67.36	1947
Wally Hardinge	2,126	54.51	1921
Les Ames	2,125	47.22	1949
Peter Richardson	2,119	38.52	1961
Frank Woolley	2,102	47.75	1914
Les Ames	2,100	61.76	1932
Arthur Fagg	2,081	41.62	1951
Peter Richardson	2,081	38.53	1962
Wally Hardinge	2,068	57.44	1922
Leslie Todd	2,057	44.71	1947
Frank Woolley	2,040	48.56	1929
Bob Wilson	2,038	46.31	1964
Arthur Fagg	2,034	39.88	1950
Bill Ashdown	2,030	41.42	1934
Arthur Fagg	2,025	43.08	1947
Wally Hardinge	2,018	42.93	1913
Frank Woolley	2,011	49.04	1931

UMPIRES

Kents Arthur Fagg, when umpiring in the England v West Indies Test match at Edgbaston in 1973, took exception to the Caribbean sides attitude when he gave Geoff Boycott not out and declined to stand at the start of the third day s play. Alan Oakman took his place but after one over, Fagg, having made his point, resumed duty.

In 1936, Claude Woolley umpired in a Kent Championship game when his brother, Frank, was playing for the hop county.

UNDERWOOD, DEREK

Derek Underwood initially played with Kent Schools before progressing to the South of England Boys XI. Even though he was born in Kent, Underwood watched his cricket at the Oval. He was later coached by Ken Barrington and Tony Lock, both of whom suggested that he was given a trial by Kent. He signed for Kent in 1962 and made his debut the following summer. It proved to be a tremendous season for him, as he headed the county averages, taking 101 wickets at 21.12 runs each. He was the youngest bowler ever to take 100 wickets in his debut season.

In 1964 Underwood once again surpassed the hundred wicket mark, taking 101 wickets at 23.52 runs apiece. It was during that season that he produced his best bowling figures of nine for 28 against Sussex at Hastings. In 1966 he headed the national first-class bowling averages, the first Kent player to do so since Colin Blythe in 1914, taking 144 Championship wickets at 12.49 runs each, with a best of nine for 37 against Essex at Westcliff. He was voted Young Cricketer of the Year and went on to make his Test debut.

The most memorable of his match-winning performances for England, for which he played 86 times, taking 297 wickets, came in 1968 at the Oval. A thunderstorm appeared to have deprived England of victory. The storm-flooded ground helped Underwood as he destroyed the Australians with a dramatic return of seven for 50. It was a great performance as the wickets had to be got against time and the odds were certainly against him

As well as taking wickets, he possessed great accuracy which tied down even the best of batsmen. In the Gillette Cup Final of 1971, Lancashire s Farokh Engineer was attempting to hit every ball on the leg side but his stroke was cramped due to over after over of unplayable length just outside his off-stump.

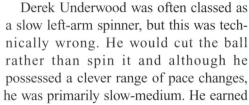

Derek Underwood.

In 1977 Underwood performed the hat-trick in the match against Sussex at Hove and the following summer he took nine wickets in an innings for the third time with nine for 32 against Surrey at the Oval. He left the Test match circuit after helping England to win the 1977 Jubilee series against Australia and in 1982 was one of the cricketers banned from Test matches for three years because he had toured South Africa with an unauthorised English team.

Derek Underwood was often classed as a slow left-arm spinner, but this was technically wrong. He would cut the ball rather than spin it and although he possessed a clever range of pace changes, he was primarily slow-medium. He earned his nickname, Deadly , by his subtle changes of trajectory and ability to get the ball almost to stand up.

In 1984 against Sussex, he hit his maiden first-class hundred — a reward for many seasons of brave and determined batting.

Derek Underwood MBE played his last game for Kent against Leicestershire in 1987. In all first-class matches he took 2,465 wickets, the fourteenth highest total of all time.

UNUSUAL DISMISSALS

In 1872, in the match against Sussex at Hove, Kent batsman George Bennett, who had not got off the mark, was given out handled ball . In

1894, Kents opening bowler Alec Hearne ran out Somersets Tyler in the match at Taunton for backing-up before he had bowled the ball.

UNUSUAL GAME

Wisden described the events of a Monday morning, the second day of the Kent v Middlesex game at Tunbridge Wells in June 1963, as: A situation without parallel in the history of first-class cricket . On the Saturday, Middlesex had dismissed Kent for 150 and ended the day on 121 for three with the not out batsmen being White (43) and Hooker (13). The Middlesex players had stayed in a local hotel for Friday night but had spent the following two nights in their own beds. On the Monday morning, the traffic was very heavy around the London Bridge area and the traffic jams reduced the chances of the players in some cars arriving in time for the 11.30 start.

Only three Middlesex players were punctual. White, one of the not out batsmen; Russell, who had already been dismissed; and Clark, the twelfth man. White changed and waited patiently on the boundary for someone to partner him. The question was how would the umpires react. There seemed a number of possibilities. Should they award the match to Kent, could the Middlesex players declare in the absence of their captain and borrow eight players to take the field or should they rule out each batsman in turn if they failed to appear within the stipulated two minutes?

The answer was none of these. The umpires officially closed the Middlesex innings.

There followed a ten minute interval before Middlesex took the field. Colin Cowdrey, the Kent captain, offered loan players to the visitors and allowed twelfth man, Clark, to keep wicket. Three more Middlesex players arrived, so only five substitutes were borrowed from Kent. One of these was Prodger and he took an excellent catch at slip in the second over to dismiss his team-mate, Brian Luckhurst. After three overs, the remaining Middlesex players arrived. Later in the innings, Prodger became one of the few players to score a fifty and take a catch in the same County Championship innings. A superb innings of 95 out of 120 in 100 minutes by Peter Richardson took Kent to a match-winning position but with rain preventing much play on the final day Middlesex escaped with a draw.

VALENTINE, BRYAN

Bryan Valentine began to play for Kent in 1927, the year after he left Repton, but it was another four years before he secured a regular place in the 1st XI line-up. In his early days he was a promising county batsman, capable of playing an entertaining and exhilarating innings with brilliant strokes, especially on the leg-side. However, he was suspect in defence.

By the mid 1930s, he had improved his defence and learned to watch the turning ball, becoming a formidable on-driver of the many off-spin bowlers that the new lbw law had produced. He still refused to be bogged down and scored at more than 50 runs per hour. The English batting at this time was strong, so his Test cricket was limited. In 1933 though, he scored 1,453 runs at 36.73 and in the close season was chosen to tour India with MCC. In the final Test at Bombay, Valentine scored 136 in under three hours.

He made the highest score of his career, 242 against Leicestershire at Oakham in 1938. In 1938-39 he toured South Africa where his consistent batting brought him an average of 45.38 including a brilliant 112 at Cape Town in the second Test.

Perhaps it is some indication of the strength in depth of the English batting before the war, that though Valentine averaged 64.85 in seven Tests against other countries, he never represented England against Australia. This was rather surprising because as well as being a high-scoring batsman, he was also a superb fielder.

After the war, during which he was awarded the MC and severely wounded, he returned to captain Kent from 1946 to 1948.

Valentine took his cricket seriously. He was as keen as anyone to win but throughout he never forgot that cricket is a game. He certainly enjoyed it himself and did his utmost to ensure that others enjoyed it too. He scored 14,131 runs for Kent at 30.52, including twenty-five centuries.

He became President of Kent in 1967 and served on the committee for many years, never losing touch with his beloved county, constantly attending Kent matches.

VICTORIES

Kents greatest number of victories in a County Championship season is twenty from twenty-eight matches in 1913 when the county won the title. Their biggest victory came in 1909 when they beat Gloucestershire at Catford by an innings and 314 runs.

WARTIME

At the outbreak of the First World War, Kent decided not to follow the lead of other counties and stop at least some of their fixtures which remained after fighting had broken out. However, the 1914 season was a financial disaster and because Dover had become an armed camp, two games at The Crabble were switched to Canterbury. The season, the most traumatic in the club s history, ended with two heavy defeats at the hands of Middlesex and Hampshire.

There was no first-class cricket for the next four years but a total of 1,382 members continued their financial contributions throughout the war which, sadly, took its toll of Kent players, the county losing eleven of its playing staff with Colin Blythe and Ken Hutchings the most notable casualties.

During the Second World War, the St Lawrence ground at Canterbury was maintained in playing condition, thus allowing the troops stationed nearby to hire it for games. The St Lawrence and Beverley clubs amalgamated to provide opposition to service sides, and at some of the matches collections for service charities were made. Also, all through the war, the spirit of Canterbury week was kept alive.

The Army occupied the county club s buildings and used the surrounds for parking ambulances, lorries and guns. There was an air raid shelter under the concrete stand and the iron stand was used as a petrol store. The St Lawrence ground was used for Home Guard training and a Women s Land Army rally was held there. More than 250 incendiary bombs fell on the ground, over half on the playing area, but the damage was negligible.

WARWICKSHIRE

Founded in 1882, Warwickshire have won the County Championship five times — in 1911, 1951, 1972, 1994 and 1995. The county won the Gillette Cup in 1966 and 1968, the Nat West Trophy in 1989, 1993 and 1995 and the Benson and Hedges Cup in 1994. They also took the Sunday League title in 1980, 1994 and 1997.

When Kent won the County Championship for the fourth time in 1913, they renewed acquaintances with Warwickshire after a gap of a number of years. At Tonbridge, Warwickshire were bowled out in their second innings for just 16, still the lowest score ever recorded against Kent. Colin Blythe and Frank Woolley each returned five for eight and the innings was over in 43 minutes and 62 balls. Kent, dismissed for 132 in their first innings, were 130 behind, but were given an unexpected chance of victory and Frank Woolley steered them to a six wicket win with an unbeaten 76.

WEST INDIES

In Kents first County Championship-winning season of 1906 they played the West Indies for the first time. The match was at Catford and Lord Harris, who had missed the last few games, returned to the side. Also recalled was Colin Blythe, who had match figures of ten for 134 as Kent beat the tourists by an innings and 14 runs.

WICKETKEEPERS

Steve Marsh equalled the then world record of eight dismissals in an innings when he took eight catches during the match against Middlesex at Lords in 1991. Les Ames holds the record for the most dismissals in a season for Kent with figures of 116 (71 caught and 45 stumped) in 1929. During the match against Northamptonshire in 1955, Kent gave away 73 extras including 48 byes in an innings. Anthony Catt, the Kent wicket-keeper was found to be suffering from sunstroke.

The following wicketkeepers have made the most dismissals in county matches for Kent:

	Played	Matches	Caught	Stumped	Total
Fred Huish	1895-1914	469	901	352	1,253
Alan Knott	1964-1985	349	828	87	915
Les Ames	1926-1951	430	512	330	842
Steve Marsh	1982-1999	291	688	61	749
Jack Hubble	1904-1929	343	411	217	628
Godfrey Evans	1939-1967	258	451	103	554
Howard Levett	1930-1947	142	227	170	397

WILSON, BOB

Always batting within his limitations and adapting himself to the conditions, Bob Wilson was a very straight batsman, yet never afraid to attack. The left-handed Wilson passed the 1,000 run mark for thirteen consecutive summers with a best of 2,038 runs at an average of 46.31 in 1964.

He was unlucky not to have played for England and he was certainly one of the best uncapped batsmen of his time. He looked good enough for a higher class of cricket — much better than some of the players who were chosen to represent their country. In 1960 he helped Arthur Phebey put on 304 for the third wicket against Glamorgan at Blackheath, and three years later he and Stuart Leary took the Northamptonshire attack apart, adding 283 for the third wicket.

This stalwart Kent batsman retired at the end of the 1967 season but from a cricketing point of view this was much too soon. In first-class matches for Kent, Wilson scored 19,458 runs at an average of 32.10.

On his retirement he became the manager of the Hastings and Thanet Building Society at Sittingbourne, later serving on the Kent General Committee.

WOOLLEY, FRANK

Frank Woolley played in his first match for Kent at Old Trafford during June 1906. It was an unusual debut to say the least. Lancashire scored 531 in just five hours with Johnny Tyldesley, who scored 295 not out, being dropped twice by Woolley, whose 26 overs and one wicket cost him 103 runs. Next day, Woolley was dismissed without scoring. In Kents second innings, Woolley batting at No.8, scored a pulsating 64 in an hour, but the red rose county won with ease. It was one of only two defeats as Kent went on to win the County Championship, Woolley scoring is maiden first-class hundred against Hampshire in his home town of Tonbridge.

Woolley made his Test debut in 1909, playing for England against Australia at the Oval. This was also the season that, along with Arthur Fielder, he set the Kent record for the tenth wicket, when they put on 235 against Worcestershire at Stourbridge. In 1910 he achieved the double for the first time, scoring 1,050 runs and taking 132 wickets. The following season, in a match against Somerset at Tunbridge Wells, he scored a century in each innings, 104 and 148 not out. During the close season tour of Australia, he scored an unbeaten 303 against Tasmania at Hobart.

As a bowler, Woolley modelled his action on Colin Blythe and in 1912, in the Oval test against Australia, he took five wickets in each of the visitors innings. In 1913 he hit his first double hundred in this country, an unbeaten 224 against Oxford University.

Frank took a keen interest in his new bats. He always had four heavy bats, each around 2lbs 6ozs, made for him — calculating that this number would cover his seasons needs. It was ironic that a man of Woolleys brilliant batting ability should be turned down by the Army during the First World War because of poor eyesight.

When cricket resumed in 1919, Woolley performed the hat-trick for the only time in his career — against Surrey at Blackheath. The following season he completed the cricketers double for the fifth time but his best remembered performance was in the Lords Test against Australia, when he held England together against Gregory and McDonald. Woolley scored 95 out of 187 and 93 out of 283, playing his strokes with plenty of time to spare against the powerful Aussies.

In 1923, Woolley hit the highest score of his career in this country— 270 against Middlesex at Canterbury. Over the next couple of seasons he hit two further double centuries — 215 against Somerset at Gravesend and 217 at Northampton. In 1928 he hit his highest number of runs in a season — 2,894 at an average of 59.06. The following season, Woolley, who had been surprisingly overlooked for the Australian tour, hit four consecutive centuries — 155 v Derbyshire at Chesterfield; 108 v Somerset at Tonbridge; 131 v Yorkshire at Tunbridge Wells and 117 v Hampshire at Folkestone.

In 1931, Woolley scored 2,011 runs, his top score being 224 against New Zealand at Canterbury. It was while compiling that score that he and Les Ames put on 277 for the fifth wicket to set a Kent record. He also completed a hundred before lunch on two occasions; the first against Surrey at Blackheath in 1930 and then three years later when Derbyshire visited Canterbury.

Woolley played first-class cricket from 1906 to 1938, scoring 58,969 runs at an average of 40.75 with 145 hundreds. For Kent, he scored 47,868 runs at 41.77 and took 1,680 wickets at 18.84 runs apiece.

After his retirement from the game he was elected a life member of the MCC and Kent and also the county committee. In the 1950s he worked at Butlins Holiday Camp, Clacton, coaching guests and organising net practice. He was quite active into his late eighties and in January 1971, he flew to Australia to watch the last two Tests. Nine months later, in Canada, he married for the second time, his first wife having died some ten years earlier.

Frank Woolley died in Halifax, Nova Scotia on 18 October 1978 at the age of ninety-one, one of the finest and most elegant of left-handed all-rounders in the history of the game.

WOOLMER, BOB

The son of a British business executive, Bob Woolmer was born in Kanpur, India, not far from the cricket ground. At the age of seven, he moved to England to begin his cricketing education at Yardley Court, Tonbridge under the guidance of A.F.Brickmore, a former Kent player

Bob Woolmer

who was headmaster of the school. Woolmer later attended Skinners School, Tonbridge and on leaving took up a post as sales representative with ICI in London. However, at the age of twenty he joined the Kent ground staff, making his first-class debut against Essex at Maidstone. He was not asked to bowl but made an unbeaten half-century.

The following summer he produced his best figures with the ball, taking seven for 47 against Sussex at Canterbury. In 1970 he was awarded his county cap and at the end of the season, he spent the winter coaching in South Africa. It was here that he perfected his bowling armoury by learning to swing the ball away. In 1972 he picked up 13 wickets in the match with Sussex (six for 70 and seven for 65). In 1975 he performed the hat-trick for the MCC against the Australians at Lords and later made his Test debut on the same ground. He was left out after his debut until the last match of the series at the Oval. He scored 149, the slowest hundred ever made by an England batsman against Australia.

In 1976 he began to open the batting for Kent and passed the 1,000 run mark in the Championship for the first time. He scored 1,461 runs at 56.19, captured more than 50 wickets and held five catches in an innings against Worcestershire to show his all-round talent.

In 1977 he scored centuries against Australia at Lords and Old Trafford. Including the Centenary Test, he had made seven appearances against the old enemy, scoring three hundreds. It equalled Peter Mays record and was better than Grace, Graveney or Woolley.

After fifteen appearances for his country, he joined the World Series Cricket founded by Kerry Packer. He did play in four further games for England in 1980 and 1981 but could not reach his original heights.

Woolmer hit the highest score of his career, 203 against Sussex at Tunbridge Wells, in 1982 before leaving the first-class scene two years later. A graceful right-handed batsman, who scored 12,634 runs at 35.09 and useful medium-fast bowler who captured 334 wickets at 23.38 runs apiece, he later managed South Africas national side to great success.

WORCESTERSHIRE

Founded in 1865, Worcestershire waited almost a century for their first title, winning the County Championship in 1964. They won it again in their centenary year of 1965; also in 1974; and in the successive years of 1988 and 1989. They have won the Sunday League three times — in 1971, 1987 and 1988; the Benson and Hedges Cup in 1991; and the Nat West Trophy in 1994.

In the match against Worcestershire at Maidstone in 1904, James Seymour wrote his name into the Kent record books when he became the first player for the county to score a century in each innings — 108 and 136 not out. The countys 10th wicket record partnership, which has stood the test of time, came in the match at Stourbridge in 1909. Going in at No.11 Arthur Fielder made an unbeaten 112, helping Frank Woolley (185) to add 235 runs in just two-and-a-half hours.

The game against Worcestershire at Tunbridge Wells in 1960 was the first County Championship match for seven years to be completed inside a day. Kent were dismissed for 187 with Peter Jones top-scoring with 73 before the visitors were bowled out for 25 (Brown six for 12 and Halfyard four for seven) and 61 (Halfyard five for 20 and Brown three for 22).

Worcestershire were Kents opponents at Canterbury for the final game of the 1972 John Player League season. Recording their sixth successive victory in the competition, the county took the title for the first time with a crowd of more than 12,000 seeing them win with two overs to spare.

WRIGHT, DOUG

In his early days, Doug Wright was thought of as a promising batsman but he did not develop in this respect. This was probably due to the fact that he was trying to work at his action. He bowled with a bounding run, often compared with a kangaroos hopping, but spun the ball hard which not all English leg-spinners did. Wrights action was certainly odd, often prone to bowling no-balls.

He made his Kent debut in 1932 and his real chance came four years later when Tich Freeman retired from the Kent side. During each of the next five seasons, excluding the war years, Wright took 100 wickets or more. In 1948, he chipped a finger and was restricted to claiming just 77 victims. Fully recovered, the following year he once again passed the 100 mark.

In 1937, Wright took two hat-tricks, at Worcester and Trent Bridge, whilst the following year he made his Test debut against Australia. In 1938-39 he toured South Africa taking yet another hat-trick at East London in the match against Border. In 1938 back home, Wright took 131 wickets at just 15.65 runs apiece including another hat-trick in figures of nine for 47 against Gloucestershire.

In 1946, Wright resumed where he had left off some seven years earlier, taking 113 wickets at 17.63. When he toured Australia in 1946-47 there was not one single Australian batsman who could master Wrights bowling. Unfortunately there were a great number of missed chances, the majority off his bowling. Wright toured Australia and South Africa twice, playing in 34 Tests in all, taking 108 wickets at 39.11.

In 1947, Wright took 142 wickets at 19.01 each. His best performance of the season being 15 for 173 against Sussex at Hastings including the fifth hat-trick of his career. Two years later he took nine for 51 against

Leicestershire at Maidstone and in the match against Hampshire at Canterbury, he took the seventh hat-trick of his career — an achievement that is currently the world record.

Wright was the first professionally appointed captain of Kent, leading the team from 1954 to 1956.

After retiring from first-class cricket, Doug Wright became professional and coach at Charterhouse. The last of the great English leg-spinners, he took 2,056 first-class wickets at an average of 23.98.

YORKSHIRE

Founded in 1863, Yorkshire won two unofficial county titles in 1867 and 1870 before going on to take the record number of thirty official championships including a sequence of four successive titles between 1922 and 1925. Until last season, Yorkshire had not tasted championship victory since 1968 when having won six of the last nine titles, they were led by Brian Close. The strong side of the 1960s won the Gillette Cup in 1966 and 1969 but until 1987 when they won the Benson and Hedges Cup, their only title came in 1983 when they won the Sunday League.

In the summer of 1904, Kent completed only one of their two games with Yorkshire — the match at Harrogate being declared void due to the wicket being tampered with. At the end of the first day, holes had appeared but by the start of the second morning, they had been filled in. There was a biggish crowd on the ground, so the game continued for their benefit, but the result did not count towards the County Championship. It must have been a big disappointment for Schofield Haigh, who had performed the hat-trick.

During the game at Sheffield in 1906, Lord Hawke of Yorkshire was bowled by Arthur Fielder but was invited by the Kent skipper to continue his innings because the bails had been blown off before the ball hit the stumps. His Lordship refused the offer.

When Kent met Yorkshire at Hull in 1924, they were trying to bat out for a draw. George Collins played a ball down to Maurice Leyland at short-leg who, though taking it low to the ground, claimed a catch. The umpire was unsighted and went to discuss the appeal with his colleague at square-leg. The Yorkshire team joined in the discussion, and George left the crease to put forward his opinion. A Yorkshire fielder removed the bails saying: You re out now . The umpire, however, declared the catch a good one.

One of the greatest catches in Kent v Yorkshire matches was taken in

134

the match at Canterbury in 1967. Kent were bidding to wrest the County Championship title away from Yorkshire, when Alan Ealham was fielding as a substitute in the deep during a tense moment in the game. Fred Trueman hit the ball a tremendous distance, and at great height. Ealham, running at full speed round the boundary, took a brilliant one-handed catch in front of the Frank Woolley stand. Trueman disputed the catch, needing several minutes of convincing that he was out.

YOUNG CRICKETER OF THE YEAR

The annual award made by the Cricket Writers Club (founded in 1946) is currently restricted to players qualified for England and under the age of twenty-three on 1 April. Four Kent players have been selected and they are:

1953	Colin Cowdrey
1965	Alan Knott
1966	Derek Underwood
1980	Graham Dilley

YOUNGEST PLAYER

The youngest cricketer to appear for Kent is Wally Hardinge who was sixteen years 111 days old when he made his debut in the County Championship match against Lancashire at Tonbridge in 1902.

ZENITH

After winning the County Championship for the first time in 1906, Woolley s first season, Kent won it again in 1909, 1910 and 1913. In between they were twice second and once third.

The county s next successful era began with the winning of the Gillette Cup in 1967. That year and the next Kent were runners-up and in 1970, their centenary year, the title justly went to Cowdrey s side — remarkably as they were bottom of the table at the beginning of July.

Kent were then in the thick of all the competitions, sharing the title with Middlesex under Asif Iqbal in 1977 and the following year, with Ealham in charge, won the Championship and the Benson and Hedges Cup for the third time.

ZIMBABWE

Kent s total of 487 for eight declared in their meeting against Zimbabwe in 2000 was their highest against a touring team since 1936 and the second-highest ever. India s Rahul Dravid s innings of 182 was the third highest maiden hundred for the county. David Masters match figures of nine for 81 were the most on a debut since 1896. This was Kent s second match against Zimbabwe and their second win.